OPEN ROAD'S BEST OF

Bermuda

by Ron Charles

Open Road Travel Guides
For the amount of time you *really* have for your trip!

Open Road Publishing

Open Road's new travel guides cut to the chase.
You don't need a huge travel encyclopedia – you need a
selective guide to steer you right. If you're going on vacation for
a few weeks or less, get a guide that brings you the *best* of any
destination for the amount of time you *really* have for your trip!

Open Road – the guide you need for the trip you want.

The New Open Road *Best Of* Travel Guides.
Right to the point.
Uncluttered.
Easy.

Open Road Publishing
P.O. Box 284, Cold Spring Harbor, NY 11724
www.openroadguides.com

Text Copyright©2009 by Ron Charles
- All Rights Reserved -
ISBN 13: 978-1-59360-120-1
ISBN 10: 1-59360-120-4
Library of Congress Control No. 2008940463

About the Author
Ron Charles is also the author of *Open Road's Best of The Bahamas*. He
makes his home in Montreal.

For photo credits and acknowledgments, turn to page 213.

CONTENTS

Your Passport to the **Perfect Trip!**

Maps

Open Road's Best Of

BERMUDA

1. INTRODUCTION

Bermuda is a beautiful island paradise. Long stretches of pink sand beaches and friendly locals set the stage for a wonderful collection of pink sand beaches, pastel cottages, world-class  seaside resorts, romantic B&Bs, superb restaurants, challenging golf courses, and typically British sensibilities. And this is one destination that never gets too hot or too cold no matter what time of year!

Bermuda offers the finest quality accommodations, cuisine, entertainment, sports and unique excursions. Several mid-sized luxury hotels and small deluxe romantic inns in every price range have sprouted up along the shoreline, the towns and in the rural countryside. Old fortresses and historic buildings have been converted into museums and public parks.

Our book has been designed to give you the information necessary to create a unique island itinerary to best match your own vacation dreams. I have also listed detailed advice and recommendations on scenic day trips, picking the perfect hotel, where to eat, available sports activities & excursions, what to shop for, where to party, and how to best get around from place to place.

Be sure to mix in a little local culture by talking with locals, and asking them for their recommendations. As a Bermudian friend once told me: *"In this world there are tourists, and then there are travelers. A tourist leaves their vacation with a bag full of T-shirts and bumper stickers. A traveler leaves with a lifetime full of experiences."*

2. OVERVIEW

Since it takes a mere two hours by airplane or only a day and a half by cruise ship to reach this beautiful nation from several major U.S. east coast cities, Bermuda has long been a favored destination for North American visitors.

Bermuda is one of the world's safest and most romantic vacation destinations. From the moment you step off the cruise ship or airplane and walk off into the dramatic Bermuda landscape, you know you have arrived somewhere special. Almost all of the nearly 66,000 citizens here, from taxi drivers to shop keepers, seem to wear a big smile and are quite happy to tell you fantastic tales or help you find your way around. If you're waiting at a bus stop, don't be surprised if a friendly stranger offers you a car ride into town. If you're asking a local's advice on a good restaurant for lunch, they may even invite you to their family seaside picnic.

In general, Bermudians are some of the friendliest people I have ever met, and are quite used to sharing their island paradise with visitors.

It's relatively easy and inexpensive to travel between several different Bermudian destinations in comfort by taxi, public bus, ferry, bicycle and motorized scooter, but rental cars simply do not exist here!

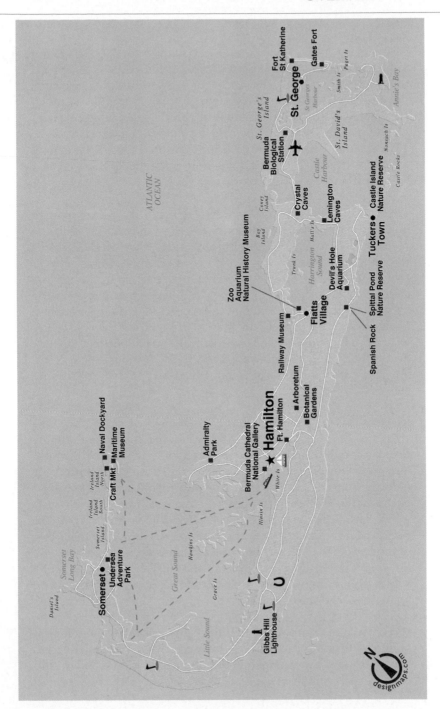

Early History

In the early 1500's – it was not uncommon for Iberian sailing vessels to be sent searching for yet another route to reach the reputed gold and spice riches of the New World. On one such voyage in 1503, **Juan de Bermudez**, captain of the Spanish vessel *La Garza*, was the first to discover this small chain of islands now has known as Bermuda. Since it first made it on to the maps in 1511, his name has ever since been identified with what is now called Bermuda. At that time the only residents of these islands were wild birds and sea creatures.

Throughout the early and middle 16th century, other Spanish and Portuguese ships were temporarily stranded on the hidden reefs that line much of the Bermuda Islands. Shipwrecked sailors from these vessels would venture ashore, only to be scared to their wits by the noises they heard after nightfall, actually the calls of wild birds, which at that time were thought of as the sounds of the Devil and his evil spirits. For many decades, Bermuda was known as **The Islands of Devils**. Almost no relics exist from these early visits, except for the so-called Spanish Rock on Bermuda's southwest shore where the initials R.P., a cross, and the date 1543 have been engraved by visiting Portuguese sailors.

In 1609, the new British colony in Jamestown, Virginia was struggling to survive with few supplies and food remaining. A fleet of nine ships from Plymouth, England was sent to re-supply Jamestown on May 15, 1609 under the direction of **Admiral Sir George Somers**. It was literally smooth sailing until the fleet encountered a sudden tempest of high seas and strong winds which struck without warning. During the storm, the 300 ton flagship known as the *Sea Venture* became separated from the rest of the pack. Over the course of the next few days, the *Sea Venture* developed a growing leak in its hull as it was carried far to the south. The strong-willed crew spent hour upon hour pumping water from the ship's hold.

As Sir George sat upon the half deck and pondered how long it would take for the vessel to sink, he spotted a small island nearby, and cried out "Land!" He then pointed the sinking wooden ship towards the coast of Bermuda, and unexpectedly ran it aground between two huge rocks not far from the shore. The wind almost immediately began to calm down, and the 150 or so men, women, and children of the ill-fated *Sea Venture* were placed along with their possessions and ship's provisions into the skiffs, and sent forward to land at what is now the coast of **St. George's**. It has been said that William Shakespeare wrote *The Tempest* based on reports of this incident.

Geography
The lovely sub-tropical paradise of Bermuda is located **in the Atlantic Ocean** at 32 degrees latitude and 64 degrees longitude, about 650 miles east of the North Carolina coastline and about 774 miles southeast of New York City. Although often mistaken as part of the Caribbean, it is actually situated much further north.

The country is made up of a collection of over 200 limestone-based islands and islets, many of which remain uninhabited, that were created by a pre-historic volcanic erup-tion. Bermuda's single largest landmass is known as **Great Bermuda Island**, which is where you will find the capital city of **Hamilton**. Several of its adjacent is-lands have been con-nected together with a series of bridges and some landfill to create the archipelago which most people refer to as Ber-muda. Together, this fish-hook shaped chain of connected islands forms a land area of more than 20 square miles and extends for some 22 miles in length, with a maxi-mum width of two miles.

This means that no matter where you stand in this nation, you are never far from the seashore.

Bermuda is best known for its **wonderful pristine beaches.** The sand here has a delightful pink hue, due to the unusual composition of calcium carbonate remains of marine invertebrates and red *Foraminifera* shell particles washed up from the extensive reefs that surround most of the islands. Many of these beaches have sheltered coves, and some are extremely isolated.

Among the most notable visitors to the shallow waters are hundreds of small colorful sub-tropical fish species that often will swim right up to you. Just offshore of Bermuda are huge fishing banks, reefs, and pelagic fisheries which host an abundant amount of jacks, marlin, tuna, shark, wahoo, snapper, grouper, mackerel, barracuda, blue marlin, and all sorts of other species. For scuba divers, snorkellers and fishermen, these areas are a source of endless adventure.

While much of Bermuda's coastline features high bluffs, bizarre geological formations and limestone boulders, the interior lands of Bermuda range from flat open spaces, to hilly areas which can reach altitudes of about 260 feet above sea level. Although agricultural and commercial development has altered much of the wild lands, there are still several remaining marsh areas, brackish ponds, subterranean caves, and nature preserves. The landscape here is home to such common flora as hibiscus, oleander, bay grape, yucca, and poinsettia, and you will also come across paw-paw, loquat, Easter lily, cassava and banana.

Due to the Gulf Stream winds, Bermuda is blessed with a superb **subtropical climate** and summer temperatures here seldom exceed 86°F. Winter is fairly mild with average daytime temperatures hovering around 68°F. Hurricanes occasionally affect Bermuda from June through November.

People
Bermuda has maintained a strong link with all things British. Most people here tend to be on the conservative side and speak with a mixture of American and English accents. They tend to

address strangers in a friendly but formal tone, and take pride in their community. As with any other country, the richer and more connected families do tend to stick together and become members of private yacht clubs and exclusive golf courses. There is an elite class here. But most Bermudians are not at all snobby.

The most popular houses of worship is the Anglican Church (Church of England) although immigrants and slaves brought with them an assortment of other faiths. As black slaves became part of the work force here in the 17th through early 19th centuries, they brought with them several religions and sects including the popular African Methodist Episcopal Church. When the Portuguese farmers came here from the Azores in the 19th century, they brought with them Roman Catholicism. There are also growing Jewish, Muslim, Seventh Day Adventist, Presbyterian, and Baptist communities.

Although racial harmony is easily witnessed in the younger generations of Bermudians, the older and more affluent white population has often been accused of minor degrees of racism. I have seen a few cases of this myself, but overall things are relatively harmonious. Currently, the population of Bermuda is about 66% black and 34% white. The average age of the 66,000 citizens is about 34 years old, and most people here have achieved at least a high school education. Although there is a fine campus at the Bermuda College, many Bermudians come to the United States and Canada for university education.

Bermuda enjoys one of the highest standards of living in the world. There is virtually no poverty, unemployment, illiteracy, and little crime or serious public health issues. With the relocation of the reinsurance industry from London to Bermuda in the 1980's, billions more dollars poured into the economy. Due to its favorable tax laws, Bermuda has also become a magnet for international banking and insurance companies looking for tax exempt status. Anybody who is educated and needs a job can easily find with one of these businesses, the huge tourism industry, or an offshoot service related field.

Now that over 600,000 tourists (mostly from America, Canada, and England) grace its shores each year, Bermuda has succeeded: tourism is the second major contributor to its rock solid economy. Since Bermuda has the second highest standard of living in the world, residents here live rather well, and don't have to pay for things like medical care and income tax.

I have summarized the highlights of Bermuda's parishes below to give you a basic idea of what each has to offer its visitors.

MAJOR ISLAND DESTINATIONS
Bermuda is officially divided into **nine parishes**. The following are brief descriptions of the major parish destinations that are covered in this book. The chapters in this guide contain detailed tips on walking tours, beach and water sports facilities, restaurant and hotel reviews, excursion possibilities, and other specific hints to help ensure that you have the trip of a lifetime!

Sandys Parish
Much of Sandys parish is quiet and tranquil. Although home to a major cruise ship port, the area is dotted with several important historic sights and various adventurous sea faring excursions. Here you can spend at one day touring a 19th-century British naval base and learn more about Bermuda's history at dramatic museums, and see local crafts being made by hand. Among the top attractions here are sunset schooner rides, reef snorkeling, Boston Whaler and sailboat rentals, several long sandy beaches, English-style pubs and popular seaside restaurants, hike trails and Segway rides along coastal nature paths, visits to centuries-old hilltop defensive forts, the world's smallest drawbridge, and the opportunity to shop till you drop – even on Sundays!

Southampton Parish
In this large parish there is lots to do. In just one day you can play a round on a championship golf course, climb to the

top of a beautiful lighthouse, suntan and socialize in the warm waters of Bermuda's most popular beaches, snorkel amidst schools of tropical fish, learn to scuba dive, walk along high bluffs and fortress walls, enjoy a refined afternoon tea, dine high atop the ocean on an open air terrace, enjoy a dinner show, and spend your nights in a room with an unforgettable view.

Warwick Parish

This part of Bermuda contains a good mixture of traditional residential neighborhoods, as well as more modern commercial zones. Warwick has some of the Bermuda's most magnificent secluded cove beaches, quaint historic churches, fine horseback riding, wild woodlands, great bird watching, family fun activities, seagoing excursions, and accommodations in all price ranges.

Paget Parish

Paget is a wonderfully beautiful area in the heart of Bermuda. Its north coast is dotted by small harbours lined with pretty Colonial mansions and cottages, and its south coast lined with even more fine beaches. This is one of the best places to visit for fantastic gardens, art galleries, sports facilities, boat rentals, cute boutiques, shipwreck diving and snorkelling cruises, action packed nightlife and entertainment, some of the islands' best restaurants, and an endless supply of hotels, inns, and apartments.

Pembroke Parish

As home to the capital city of **Hamilton**, Pembroke parish is the heart of Bermuda. You can easily spend several days in this parish just exploring both its cosmopolitan and rural sights. Here you can take a carriage ride past the pastel color storefronts, hop on a glass bottom boat, shop for great bargains, view internationally renowned artwork, dance in the streets during festivals, visit museums, watch Parl-

18 OPEN ROAD'S BEST OF BERMUDA

iamentary proceedings, witness traditional skirling ceremonies, head to the seaside nature reserves, indulge in participant and spectator sports, enjoy exotic restaurants and party all night long.

Devonshire Parish
Now you are in a delightfully tranquil area of the country. Here you won't find many of the same distractions and development which is common elsewhere. This is the perfect place to go and enjoy rural Bermuda and its lush terrain. Besides wonderful walking trails, here your kids can learn English style horseback riding, play an inexpensive round of golf, hit the squash courts, bird watch in an Audubon sanctuary, picnic in peaceful seaside parks, and tour the windswept hamlets of the north coast.

Smith's Parish
This parish has a vast array of unusual geological wonders, natural beauty, and a few quiet beaches. You can wander through an old pirate haven, witness strange checkerboard rock formations, see inscriptions left by early European explorers, tour an opulent 18th century mansion, take an exciting helmet dive to the bottom of the sea, walk Cliffside trails at water's edge, and stumble upon unusual creatures in nature reserves.

Hamilton Parish
In this part of Bermuda there are dozens of memorable sights and attractions, many of which are within easy walking distance of each other. There is a wonderful aquarium, an impressive zoo, several museums, a perfume factory, a glass blowing workshop and studio, amazing caves with stalactites and stalagmites, fun places to stop for anything from a milk shake to a rum swizzle, excellent world class resorts and golf courses, tons of water sports activities including jet skiing and scuba diving.

St. George's Parish
This easternmost part of Bermuda was where this nation was first settled. Some of the many great things to see in both the old city of St. George and its surroundings include fine examples of early Bermudan architecture, boutique-laden historic lanes, magnificent beaches, posh residential areas, hilltop defensive batteries, museums depicting life in the old days, fine art galleries, beauti-

ful seaside parks, a wonderful old lighthouse, a couple of the most authentic Bermudan restaurants, challenging golf courses, and great pubs and taverns.

3. HAMILTON

Located on a wide peninsula that juts out from **Great Bermuda Island** into the sea, **Pembroke** is this nation's busiest and most often gridlocked parish. Originally named after the third Earl of Pembroke, about 24 percent of Bermudians live here.

With a huge assortment of fine shops, restaurants, nightclubs, pubs, hotels, charming inns, sights and museums, **Hamilton** is the most logical starting point of your journey through this parish. The various towers of churches and government buildings in the heart of the city can be seen from far away; when cruise ships dock alongside Front Street they are good landmarks to use while navigating around town. And just outside of town there are many **wonderful back roads and mansion-lined country lanes** that are perfect for half-day walks and rides.

ONE GREAT DAY IN HAMILTON

No scooters, public buses or taxis are required for this tour, but if you want to get around by scooter, note that while parking can be found on every major street in town, the 350 or so dedicated curbside moped spaces tend to fill up fast. Be persistent because after a few attempts you will find an open spot with free parking. You should be able to see all the sights in this pretty little city in one full day.

MORNING
Front Street
Since most people visiting Hamilton tend to arrive by ferry, I will start the walking tour from the harbor front Hamilton **Ferry terminal** where you will find payphones and a 24 hour ATM bank machine. From here you can cross the street and turn right onto historic **Front Street** passing by **A.S. Cooper & Sons** clothing shop as well as the **Irish Linen** shop. Although dozens more fine boutiques, restaurants, pubs, and nightclubs can be found in the pretty pastel-colored buildings that line the upcoming section of Front Street, we will save them for a bit later on this tour.

During the high season, two huge cruise ships moor themselves at the wharfs along this street and release thousands of additional tourists who spill out in droves onto this normally manageable main city street.

Queen Street
At this point you should have reached the first major intersection, where you'll turn left (north) onto Queen Street. Just before turning, you can't help but notice the round **Birdcage** traffic box platform in the middle of the intersection. During rush hour you may find a uniformed policeman (complete with Bermuda shorts) directing traffic and gladly posing for photos.

As you head up on the left (west) side of Queen Street, you will first pass by the **Bermuda Book Store**, owned by the Zuill family whom are noted historians and authors in their own right. If you are looking for either current bestsellers or special interest books to help identify local geography, wildlife, history, and culture, then this is the place. Next is the quaint **Island Shop** specializing in decorative arts, then the huge **Riihiluoma's Flying Colors** T-shirt shop, and the adorable little **Scottish Wool Shop** where I picked up a couple of fantastic Shetland sweaters for less than $30 each. Also worthy of mention is the **Lemon Tree Café** a superb lunch venue with an outdoor terrace and superb cuisine.

Now you'll wander past the entrance to Hamilton's most serene attraction, the **Par-La-Ville Park**. This wonderful palm and shrub-filled public park was once the private garden of fabled Bermu-

Let Me Take You on a Sea Cruise!

The small docks next to the Visitors Ferry Terminal are the departure slips for several **sea excursions**. Among the vast assortment of exciting adventures (usually from April through November only) that leave from these docks are the following, in order of my recommendations:

•**Hayward's Snorkeling & Glass Bottom Boat Cruises** – fantastic 3-hour morning and afternoon trips daily on a 54' motor yacht for $38 per person including all the necessary gear.

• **Sail Bermuda** – take a peaceful half-day or sunset outings aboard their beautiful sailing yachts each day for $35 per person and up.

•**Bermuda Water Tours** – several unique excursions each week including a full day lunch cruise for $40 per person which lets its clients not only snorkel and swim along the way, but also includes a full lunch at the Waterside Inn and admission fees to the Maritime Museum at the Dockyard.

•**Reef Roamers** – twice daily on a 2-hour glass bottom boat trips (high season only) to the sea gardens and a shipwreck for $40 per person.

•**Bermuda Island Cruises** – tacky theme dinner-cruise excursions like their Pirate Party Night with entertainment and a dinner buffet for $65 per person each Tuesday, Wednesday, Friday, and Saturday at 7pm.

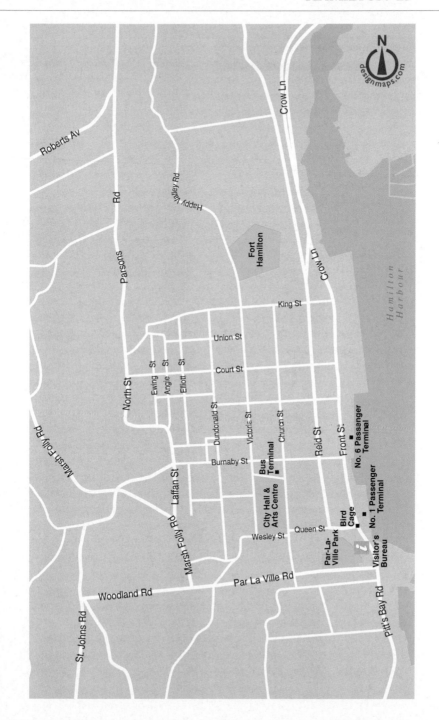

Don't Miss ...

- Front Street
- Wednesday's Harbour Night
- Bermuda Underwater Exploration Institute
- Par-La-Ville Park
- Perrot Post Office
- Fairmont Hamilton Princess Hotel
- Fort Hamilton

dian postmaster William Bennet Perot. His lovingly manicured gardens of exotic plants and trees have become a peaceful location for both businessmen and tourists alike to relax and enjoy box lunches upon its many benches. As you wander through the lovely stone-topped trails and peaceful gardens it is hard to believe that you are actually in the middle of a bustling city. The park also has public restrooms and nearby pay telephones for your added convenience. Admission to the park is free, and it is open daily from sunrise to sunset.

The next building you'll pass is the **Perot Post Office**, a cute two-story 19th century building shutters and cedar beams is Bermuda's first official post office. Bermuda's original postmaster, William Bennet Perot, would greet arriving sea vessels at the wharfs to get the incoming mail, and then walk around town to personally deliver these letters. In 1848 he decided to print and sign Bermuda's first stamps to further minimize his workload, and assure that the correct postage was paid for outgoing letters. Less than a dozen of these highly valued original hand-signed stamps still exist today. This fine example of Bermudian architecture still operates as a branch post office complete with an original antique wooden counter, extremely friendly and patient postal employees, oil paintings of Mr. Perot and Queen Victoria, and sometimes lines of tourists who pay 60 cents to mail their cards and letters back to America. *Info*: The post office is open from 9am until 5pm weekdays, and admission is free.

A few meters (yards) up from the post office, you will see a large rubber tree that Mr. Perot planted here, in his house's front yard, from a seed in 1847. His former home has become the **Bermuda Library & Historical Society Museum** building. The library itself offers a vast reference section full of rare historical books about Bermuda, and a full range of more modern reference and reading materials. Non-Bermudians may be permitted to withdraw books here if they inquire upstairs.

The three-room museum exhibit area displays a series of antiques and artifacts including paintings of the founders and former governors of Bermuda, 18th century European furniture, scale models of the Sea Venture, beautiful old clocks, antique coins, 17th century maps of Bermuda, old Bermudian family heirlooms, and if you inquire with the staff, perhaps they will let you take a peek at the 1775 letter from George Washington written to the inhabitants of Bermuda asking for help in obtaining gunpowder for the Revolutionary War. Unfortunately, most of the exhibits have no descriptive plaques. *Info*: The library is open from 9:30am until 6pm Monday through Friday, and until 5pm on Saturday and admission is free. The museum is open from 9:30am until 12:30pm and 2pm until 4:30pm Monday through Saturday and a $2 donation is requested.

Across the street from the library is **David Winston**, a superb men's clothing retailer with fine imported linen and cotton garments as well as Italian suits.

Further along Queen Street you should pop in for a bit of browsing and window shopping on the way to the next cultural attraction. Directly across Queen Street from the Bermuda Library you should first take a peek in the **Windsor Place** mall. Inside the mall there are a few boutiques including a back entrance to the huge **Phoenix Pharmacy Centre** which sells everything from cold remedies and film to books and toys, a 24-hour ATM bank machine, the second floor **Air Canada** reservations and ticketing offices, a 24-hour ATM bank machine and a pay phone.

A bit further up this side of Queen Street you will find a few more places worth a good look at, including the fantastic **Crissons** jewelers where I have found some serious bargains on Swiss watches, one-of-a-kind European gold bracelets, and cute sterling pendants.

A couple of doors further up you will first pass by the **Little Theater** with its twice daily screenings of first run American movies, and a rather odd pari-mutuel betting parlor appropriately named **Sea Horses Turf Accountants**.

City Hall & Arts Centre

Now that you are at the intersection, cross the street and make a right turn onto the far (north) side of **Church Street**. On the next block you are confronted by the impressive circular driveway, charming fountains, white Bermudian style facade, and towering bronze Sea Venture-topped weather vane of **City Hall & Arts Centre**, designed in the late 1950's by Wilfred Onions. From the minute you step inside this fine building's massive cedar doors, you are surrounded by elaborate chandeliers, impressive paneling, and portraits of Queen Elizabeth and former mayors which are all protected by remarkably cold air conditioning. During the summer I have spent hours at a time here to escape the blistering heat.

Several side rooms contain small local exhibits like the **Benbow Stamp Collection**, an intimate theater that hosts live music events, and private municipal government offices including those of the mayor. Upstairs you will find some of the most incredible works of art to be found in all of Bermuda. *Info*: City

CITY HALL & ARTS CENTRE

Hall is open from 9am until 5pm Monday through Friday, and 9am until 12noon on Saturdays, and admission is always free. Public restrooms are available at this location.

The **East Wing** on the second floor of City Hall is home to the **Bermuda National Gallery**.

Admission is now free for all who enter. This dramatic gallery houses several outstanding collections of fine art. The first installation of art works is the Herewald T. Watlinton Collection, named after a local millionaire who willed his private collection to Bermuda. This permanent exhibit contains 18 wonderful European paintings from artists such as Gainsborough, Murillo, Romney, Palma Vecchio, de Vos, and others.

Last, but certainly not least, is the upstairs **West Wing** of City Hall, which has become the home of the **Bermuda Society of Arts Gallery**. This is a more informal collection of the society's local member artists' best work. Since the exhibits are constantly changing, you may be able to view local watercolors, oil paintings, photography, sculptures, modern stained glass, and batik works. *Info*: Admission to this gallery is free and is open from 10am until 4pm from Monday to Saturday.

Further Along Church Street
After departing City Hall, continue walking down the same side of Church Street until you have reached the next corner. Here you can't help but notice the **Central Bus Terminal**, home base of all public bus routes through Bermuda. If you need any tokens, tickets, passes, directions, or transit maps, then you really should stop here.

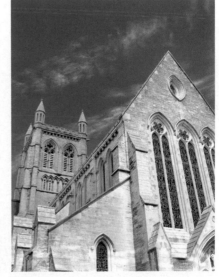

Two blocks further down (east) on Church Street is the unmistakable Neo-Gothic tower and facade of the **Cathedral of the Most Holy Trinity**. This outrageously ornate Anglican church is also known to locals as the **Bermuda Cathedral**. This huge church, designed by William Hays of Scotland, was inspired by several 8th-12th century English cathedrals and was finally completed in 1911 using limestone, granite, and marble from all over the world. Inside this house of prayer you will find many treasures including hand-carved oak pews with locally embroidered cushions, dramatic stained glass windows, beautifully carved choir stalls, and a memorable marble altar. *Info*: The Cathedral is open daily from 8am until 6pm and admission is free.

Heading further down (east) on Church Street, the next place you may wish to see is the **Bermuda Department of Tourism** office at 43 Church Street in the building known as Global House. After you have passed by the security guard in the lobby, he will direct you to the office where you can pick up dozens of different free maps, calendars of events, tourist brochures, hotel guides, golf guides, and other useful literature.

At the next corner is the oldest church in town, **St. Andrew's Presbyterian Church**. Built in 1846, this Neo-Gothic structure was constructed on land donated by then-Governor Lieutenant Colonel William Reid. Over the years several new additions have been added including its bold organ and choir chancel, bell tower, and administration offices. *Info*: Open from 8am until 7pm daily; no fee.

Court Street

Now you are at the intersection of Court Street, where you will be taking a right (south) turn and walking down its right-hand (west) side. On the top of the hill somewhat hidden by a massive whitewashed wall is the massive 19th century **Sessions House** which was originally completed in 1817, with the Italian-inspired terra cotta **Jubilee Clocktower** and colonnade added in the later part of the 19th century. During much of the year, the **House of Assembly** sessions take place on the top floor.

With its Old World English-style proceedings and customs, you may want to take a few hours out of your day to watch one of these meetings from the upstairs visitors' gallery. When no session is taking place, the Sergeant at Arms might just open the chambers for you to look at if asked politely. The lower floor is home to Bermuda's **Supreme Court**, which also invites the general public to watch the robed and wigged participants argue their cases from a visitor's gallery. *Info*: Call 292-7408 to find out if a House of Assembly or Supreme Court session is scheduled while you're in town; watching this is a great once in a lifetime experience. The building itself is open to the public from 9am until 5pm on weekdays, and admission is free. During the low season, a free 30 minute guided walking tour through the Sessions House is hosted by a clerk of the House of Assembly at 11:15am on most Mondays. An in-depth discussion of Parliament's role in making Bermudian laws and policy is held during and immediately following the tour.

Fort Hamilton
Retrace your steps (north) back up Court Street until again reaching the intersection of Church Street, where you will turn right (east). After following Church Street for another two blocks or so, you will come to a dead end where you should turn left (north) onto King Street towards the back end of town. After a block or so you will find a sharp uphill turnoff on the right (east) side of the road onto **Happy Valley Road**, which you will follow for a few minutes uphill until finally reaching Fort Hamilton Drive which leads directly to the entrance of **Fort Hamilton**.

This restored 19th century fort was ordered to be built by the Duke of Wellington to protect Hamilton from attack. Although never used in any battle to defend the city, its massive angular fortifications, slat-house, shrub filled moats, stone tunnels, and 1 ton gun placements are a perfect spot to get a great panoramic view over the downtown waterfront area. During the restoration process, much of the fort's landscaping was altered slightly to accommodate gardens and a large green. *Info*: The fort is open from 9:30am until 5pm Monday through Friday, and admission is free.

Back to Front Street
After a good walk around the fort, wander back over to King Street, turn left (south),

Bagpipes at the Fort

During low season, the traditionally dressed **Bermuda Isles Pipe Band** hosts a bagpipe and skirling ceremony on the fort's lush green each Monday at noontime. This is without doubt the best time to visit the fort.

The Bermuda Festival

Each winter between the first week of January and the last week of February, Hamilton hosts the famous **Bermuda Festival**. This is one of those special events that brings out all of Bermuda's leading citizens in a show of support for the arts. Events range from casual jazz concerts and art exhibitions, to more dressy events like chamber music recitals and theatrical performances by world renowned artists. If you happen to be planning a stay in town during these weeks, make sure you call well in advance for these tickets. Prices generally range from $30 to $60 for regular events, $75 or so for gala evenings, and students can receive up to 40% off. Events take place at the City Hall Theater and several other locations around Hamilton. For schedules, prices, reserved advance seating, and further information call the festival organizers at Tel. 441/295-1291. These shows are an excellent way to spend a few evenings, and perhaps meet some interesting new friends from the local community.

and follow it down all the way to its end at the intersection of Front Street. As you turn right (west) onto Front Street, walk for another block or so; you'll pass several eating and drinking establishments including the **Docksider Pub** and the popular **Double Dip** ice cream parlour.

At the next corner you will find the gates surrounding the understated **Cabinet Building**. This fine mansion-style building dates back to 1838, and now houses the offices of the extremely personable Premier of Bermuda, Sir John Swan, and his cabinet. This is the scene of several serious closed-door Cabinet meetings each month. The **Senate** also meets here, with the general public invited to view its weekly Wednesday sessions. The building contains several beautiful antiques and portraits. On the front lawn is a huge limestone **Cenotaph**, dedicated to those Bermudians who perished during World Wars I and II. The Cabinet Building is open to the public from 9am until 5pm on weekdays, and admission is free.

AFTERNOON

After departing the Cabinet Building, keep heading west on Front Street, Hamilton's most important shopping road. Since it is probably a good time to grab a bite and rest for a while, soon you will pass several great places to eat, drink, and shop 'till you drop. In order of what you will be seeing while heading west on this block of Front Street (between **Parliament Street** and **Burnaby Street**), these are a few of my favorite spots to pop into: the **Bermuda Bistro** restaurant, the **Bolero** bistro, the **Level** disco, **Swiss Timing** watch shop, **Café Cairo** restaurant and late night club, and **Davison's of Bermuda** t-shirt shop, Just off to the right is a quaint pedestrian only side street known as **Chancery Lane** (with several small boutiques and moderately priced bistro style restaurants including **Fresco's** and **Bistro J**).

Harbour Nights

On Wednesday evenings during the summer from 7pm until about 10pm, all of Front Street is closed off to vehicles for the enchanting **Harbour Night** street festivals. These harbour nights attract locals and tourists of all ages who wish to socialize and wander over towards street side vendors selling local handicrafts, stalls serving spicy Caribbean food, amusing sidewalk fashion shows, excellent live bands, and extended store opening hours (some close after 9pm). This is a highly enjoyable experience for adults and kids alike. Try to attend at least one Harbour Night if you are here during high season.

The very next block of Front Street (between Chancery Lane and Burnaby Street) takes you past **Astwood Dickinson** jewelry store, **Carole Harding** arts and crafts shop, **Onion Jacks** souvenir shop, **Making Waves** swimwear, the opulent but affordable **Crissons** jewelry boutique, the **Emporium Mall** that contains the vastly popular **Flanagan's** Irish pub (with live or dj music most nights) as well as a rather helpful branch of the **Visitor's Information Cemtre** where maps and general tourist advice are available. Also on the street is a small mall called **Butterfield Place** with a 24 hour **ATM** bank machine and a high-end **Louis Vuitton** boutique.

The following block (between Burnaby Street and Queen Street) is home to **Front Street Wines**, **MaxMara** women's apparel, a good Thai restaurant called **Silk**, the **Pickled Onion** bar and grill, the **A.S. Cooper** crystal and porcelain shop, **Lusso** fine European leather goods, the **English Sports Shop**, **Calypso** women's wear, and then **Brown & Co.**, an upscale department store (now open on Sundays from 1pm-5pm) containing three floors of the finest quality imported fragrances, women's clothing, and unique gift items. On the second floor of Brown & Co. is a delightful café known as the **Birdcage Café** which offers up light snacks and

afternoon tea with a wonderful view out over the harbor. And then on the corner is **Goslings**, my favorite liquor and wine shop in Bermuda (*photo on left*).

Now Up to Reid Street

If you have some extra time to shop, I suggest a walk up to **Reid Street**, which is just behind and runs parallel to Front Street. On the first couple of blocks on the far (north) side of this large commercial street you will find such retail business as the **Harbourmaster** luggage and leather goods shop and the main entrance to the **Phoenix Centre** pharmacy, just before the **Washington Mall**. This mall has several good shops including the **Tie Deck**, the **Mall Magazines** kiosk, the **Mall Photo Studio**, and the **London Beauty Clinic**.

A bit further down the street you will also run into the **Yankee Store** gift shop and the **Bermuda Railway Co.** clothing store. On the near (south) side of Reid Street there's the **Aston & Gunn** and

Stephanel clothing shops, and another branch of the superb **Crissons** jewelry shop.

The Bermuda Underwater Exploration Institute (B.U.E.I.)

Located on the edge of Hamilton Harbour just alongside East Broadway (not far from downtown Hamilton's bustling Front Street) is the **Bermuda Underwater Exploration Institute**. This state of the art multimedia museum has become one of the islands' most popular and interesting venues for adults and children of all ages. B.U.E.I. is housed in a brand new two-floor waterside complex that has been specially designed to enclose dozens of special self-guided interactive exhibits that explore the past, present, and future of sea exploration along the reefs that surround Bermuda.

The first exhibit, known as **"The Ocean Revealed,"** focuses attention on the effects of the ocean on the rest of the planet. Among the more interesting elements on display here are exhibits showing the effects of undersea pressure on humans and machines, examples of early helmet diving and scuba gear, deep sea submersibles, and a full scale replica of the Bathysphere that was used by Drs. Beebe and Barton to descend a record breaking 3,028 feet below the surface back in 1934.

The next exhibit space you will encounter will be **"Underwater Bermuda"** which among other topics will also explain once and for all just why the sand along much of Bermuda is pink, and then compares it with sand samples from other famous beaches in America, Europe, Hawaii and Australia. Further along is the **"Lightbourn Shell Room"** which is lined by beautifully lit glass cases filled with an awesome collection of sea shells.

After leaving the shell collection you are then guided towards **"The Dive,"** a twenty-seat multimedia deep sea capsule descent simulator. Before

entering the simulator, you will be shown a video narrated by author/diver Peter Benchley that will explain some of what to expect to see along your "voyage" until reaching a virtual sea bottom some 12,000 feet below. Upon entering the ride you will be seated and then briefed before the three-minute ride begins. Several video monitors display views outside the capsule as well as simulated readings from various navigational systems. As the narrated "descent" begins you will feel movement and a change in depth as, at various depths, you can run across whales, jellyfish, sharks, and even giant squid, which are displayed across a large video screen. For adults and kids alike the ride is perhaps the most exciting part of you adventure at B.U.E.I.

On the lower level of the building and proceed into "The Sea Floor" exhibit. Here you can listen to the sounds of marine animals at several state of the art listening posts, study an echo sonar chart of the sea floor, and play an amusing interactive laser guided game called laser diver. Next on the agenda are a series of rooms called "The Reef Area and Shipwreck Gallery" that display locations and historical data about famous shipwrecks, artifacts and antiquities found nearby by famed Bermudian treasure hunter Teddy Tucker, from other local wrecks.

The Bermuda Underwater Exploration Institute is a privately funded non-profit organization whose international advisory board includes famous marine biologists, treasure hunters such as Teddy Tucker, and renowned divers such as Peter Benchley (of "Jaws" fame). There is also a wonderful gourmet restaurant anf suoerb Sushi Bar known as **Harbourfront** serving fantastic lunches and dinners daily, boutiques and logo shops, plenty of free parking, wheelchair accessible ramps and elevators, and volunteer guides to explain various elements of the submerged world. *Info*: B.U.E.I. is open from 10am until 50pm daily and has an admission fee of $12.50 per adult, $10 for senior citizens, $6 for children between 7 and 12 years of age, and is free for kids 6 and under when accompanied by an adult. Guided tours conducted by B.U.E.I. volunteers are scheduled on Tuesdays at 10:30am. For more details please contact BUEI at Tel. 441/292-7219, or visit their website at www.buei.org.

EVENING

After a long full day of walking around the city of Hamilton a good dinner has been well deserved. Since at this point you are already at B.U.E.I. you may want to consider popping into the Sushi Bar at **Harbourfront** which is right on premises. Other great dinner choices would include walking over to nearby **Café Cairo** or **Silk** or **Little Venice** or perhaps taking a taxi or a scooter over to either **Ascots** or the **House of India**. In any case, call first to make a reservation!

After dinner I suggest enjoying a cocktail over at one of the area's many pubs, bars, and wine bars such as **Robin Hood, The Pickeld Onion, Flanagan's, The Hog Penny, Fresco's Wine Bar** or the ultra-hip **Café Cairo.**

TGIF!

On Fridays at 5pm during the summer, many Hamilton executives and visitors alike head straight for the superb outdoor harbor-view terrace for **happy hour at the Hamilton Princess hotel**. Located just a few blocks away from Front Street on Pitt's Bay Road, it's the city's best palace to enjoy a beer or a cocktail and chat with plenty of well-dressed locals. There is no cover charge, drink prices are reasonable (you need to buy beverage coupons from dedicated kiosks) and there are usually at least a few hundred people that congregate here before sunset is over and then head off to the city's other night spots.

4. THE SOUTH SHORE

Bermuda's south shore contains a large section of **Southampton Parish**, a long thin curved strip of hilly land surrounded by the Atlantic Ocean to the south and the Great Sound to the north; as well as dramatic seaside cliffs and beaches along southern parts of **Warwick Parish**, **Paget Parish**, and **Devonshire Parish**.

Come to the south shore to relax in the sun and splash in the water, play golf or tennis, or just enjoy the beautiful scenery.

A WEEKEND ON THE SOUTH SHORE

If you have already visited Hamilton and you are now in need of some sun & sand, here is a tour of Bermuda's **best beach, park and garden destinations on the beautiful south shore**. Use of a public bus, taxi, or rental scooter will be required for this tour.

DAY 1
Morning
I would suggest starting just after a late breakfast, and hop in a public bus or taxi or scooter and head straight for the vast string of unforgettable beaches along Bermuda's famed south shore in both **Southampton** and **Warwick parishes**. Don't forget to bring the essentials including your cash, sunscreen, bathing suit, beach towels, camera(s), snorkel gear, and perhaps a bottle or two of ice cold beverages.

For this trip, start at the western edge of South Road, over in Southampton at the **Church Bay Beach**, the first in a string of awesome beaches, many of which are rung by silky pink sand, quaint coves and dramatic rock formations. This small hillside cove beach is a great spot to relax and enjoy shallow water snorkeling.

After a couple of hours snorkeling at Church Bay, continue east along South Road for another 750 yards (750 meters) or so and stop for a peek over at **The Reefs** hotel, a romantic and lavishly

Snorkeling at Church Bay

The first of several beaches with seaside parks along this section of South Road is the great little **Church Bay Beach**. This is one of Bermuda's best coastal snorkeling areas and consists of a small beach with a rocky ocean floor that attracts an amazing array of semi-tropical fish. There are no real facilities here (and no restrooms), so bring your own snorkeling gear and food or drink. No admission to this beach. There is also a bus stop at the entrance.

appointed small luxury hotel offers what may be some of the finest sea-front hotel accommodations and million dollar timeshare units in Bermuda. The Reefs' wonderful private cove beach, limestone moon-gate, opulent outdoor terraces and rock-lined walking paths are all worth a peek.

Afternoon
While you are at The Reefs anyway, consider enjoying a superb Bermudian-fusion lunch at the hotel's awesome **Coconuts** cliff-side bistro terrace. This unique casual dining venue offers with some of the best sea-views on earth.

For those on tighter budgets, just 300 meters (300 yards) further east along South Road is a well known restaurant, bar, gourmet deli & vintage wine shop known as **Henry VIII**. Besides offering fresh sandwiches and cool beverages to go in the pantry section, the bar at Henry VIII is famed for the Staff Night parties which are the place to hang out and both drink and dance with the workers from many of Bermuda's nearby hotels and restaurants as they end their unrelenting work week late on Sunday evenings. This is also a great place to stop in for food and beverage supplies if you prefer a more affordable al fresco afternoon picnic!

Nearby is a winding lane called Lighthouse Road where you should turn left onto and head up for some 350 meters (350 yards) before turning left again onto St. Anne's Road for another 300 meters (300 yards) to reach the entrance road for the towering **Gibbs Hill Lighthouse**. This white

Don't Miss ...

- Horseshoe Bay Beach
- Church Bay Beach
- Gibbs Hill Lighthouse
- The Reefs
- South Shore Park
- Elbow Beach
- Bermuda Botanical Gardens

tower was first constructed in England and then shipped over and reassembled on this sight in 1846. Typically packed with bus and taxi excursion passengers struggling to climb its 185 narrow steps to the top, this huge cast iron lighthouse stretches out atop the tallest hill in Bermuda to reach its peak at over 362 feet above sea level. A self-guided walk brings visitors up to a narrow panoramic lookout platform (not for those with weak knees) with unsurpassed views out over the entire country. *Info*: The lighthouse is open from 9am until 4:30pm daily and costs $2.50 to enter. The tower is closed in February.

After returning to South Road, keep heading east along the coast for another 750 meters (750 yards) until passing by the entrance gateway to the famous **Fairmont Southampton Princess Hotel** (*photo below*). On the opposite side of the road you will also see the **Fairmont Southampton Beach and Tennis Club**, which is also the site of a good seafood restaurant. Just opposite on the left hand side of the road you will see the stunning 18 hole par 54 executive **Southampton Golf Course** which can be enjoyed with advance reservations for around $84 person including golf cart rental, or $65 per person including cart after 3pm. Just behind the golf area is the towering facade of the deluxe Fairmont Southampton Princess Hotel with a host of world-class facilities including the posh **Newport Room** which is the island's only 5-

Crabs on Parade!

Although small red land crabs (Gecarcinus Lateralis) may occasionally try to steal your lunch while enjoying a picnic or outdoor meal along the south shore beaches, these crabs put on a much more dramatic yearly demonstration of Mother Nature's powers. A swarm consisting of tens of thousands of spawning crabs converge across South Road for a handful of nights after each full moon during July and August in order to reproduce near the beachfront. Even though countless hundreds of these small crunchy animals get squashed to death by passing cars, scooters, and hungry seabirds, more than enough of them make it to the beach in one piece to ensure the species' future survival.

diamond rated restaurant, as well as one of Bermuda's best and most romantic gourmet restaurants known as the **Waterlot Inn**. This unique dining venue is among my favorites and serves up some of Bermuda's finest steaks, lobster, fresh fish, and a wide array of simply outstanding Continental cuisine in the romantic setting of a 300-year old converted Captain's house filled with antiques.

From the Southampton Princess, follow South Road until passing the first in a series of amazing pink sand beaches that are known all over the world. Most of the following local beaches are part of a wonderful seaside recreation area known as **South Shore Park**. The park has various walking paths that interconnect an enchanting chain of adjacent picturesque beach areas from one to one another.

The most famous of these great beaches is the long and sandy crescent shaped **Horseshoe Bay Beach**, often seen gracing the covers of many travel guides and magazines. The beach is well equipped to deal with the hundreds of sunbathers that flock here on hot summer days and boasts dramatic cliffs, enchanting sea-rock formations, public changing rooms and showers, bathrooms, beach chair rental kiosks, free scooter and bicycle parking, payphones, and lifeguards during the summer months. There is a public bus stop located about 600 meters (600 yards) uphill from the base of the beach.

The beach is open from sunrise to sunset daily, and just like all public beaches in Bermuda, there is no admission fee. While Horseshoe Bay Beach is  a great place to socialize and offers plenty of "activity" during the high season, the smaller and more intimate beaches that follow are far less crowded! Also on the beach is the great little **Horseshoe Bay Beach House** where you can enjoy moderately priced sandwiches and snack foods or ice cream at one of many indoor or outdoor tables from about 10am until around 7pm in the warmer months.

The nearby cliff-top trails are well worth the effort to explore, and they all lead out in various directions within the zone known as **South Shore Park**. The park contains an additional selection of equally impressive but less busy secluded cove beaches towards the east with names like **Peel Rock Cove, Butts Beach, Middle Beach, Wafer Rocks Beach, Angle Beach, Chaplin Bay Beach, Stonehole Bay Beach** and **Jobson's Cove Beach**. These spots are good places for romantic evening walks. All of the beaches in and around South Shore Park are also open all day long and have no admission fees. A few hours of wandering around these trails and adjacent beaches are the perfect way to enjoy an afternoon by the sea.

As you cross over from Southampton Parish into Warwick Parish either the Cliffside paths of South Shore Park or via bus or taxi or scooter on the scenic South Road, you'll see the continuation of **South Shore Park**, with still more great beaches. This part of the enchanting seaside park contains some of the prettiest and most tranquil beaches imaginable, including (from west to east) the cute grottos of **Stonehole Bay**, the calm sheltered waters at **Jobson's Cove**, and the shrub and grassy hills that stretch the full length of fantastic **Warwick Long Bay**. As its name suggests, the windy pink sand beach at Warwick Long Bay is rather long (perhaps the longest stretch of beach in Bermuda), and contains public restrooms and lots of parking – but lifeguards are not on duty here since the undertow is not all that strong. These are all great places to enjoy the sun and sand in relative isolation.

About another 1.5 kilometers (1500 yards) further east down South Road from Warwick Long Bay is a right side entrance road to the beautiful **Astwood Park**. This park is one of my favorite picnic and hiking areas, which also has the added benefit of the small secluded **Astwood Park Beach** surrounded by a series of cliffs that are home to several Longtail bird nests. The park and beaches are always open, and admission is free. Public restrooms can be easily found near the beach area. Just next to Astwood Park is the much more private **Marley Beach**.

Evening
After leaving the beaches of this area, have a great (and afford-able) dinner on the outdoor patio of the laid-back **The Swizzle** bar & restaurant, just across the street on South Road. For those of you with considerably higher dinner budgets, you may want to consider ending your evening just before sunrise at the fantas-tic **Lido Restaurant** at the nearby Elbow Beach hotel's private beachfront. In either case, after a long day of beaches and other attractions, you may be tired and will probably want to head back to your room for a rest before considering what nightlife best suits you.

DAY 2
Morning
Today you may want to get up a bit early and head off to see some more beaches, gardens, and other attractions in Paget and Devonshire parishes. Once again you can hop on a bus, taxi or scooter an head for the next part of South Road in Paget parish.

Your first stop should be the luxurious **Elbow Beach Hotel**. Besides being my favorite large seaside resort hotel in Bermuda, this fine deluxe resort offers several dozen breathtak-

ing acres of enchanting sea view grounds.

Some of the most memorable facilities on the Elbow Beach Hotel's property is the amazing **Seaside Terrace** dining complex, which also houses **Restaurant Lido** and **Mickey's** beachside cafe. Lido is one of the island's best places to enjoy top of the line Italian influenced steak and pasta dishes as well as some of the best local and imported grilled seafood. The terrace's new outdoor tapas bar and cocktail lounge is also a great choice for more casual snacks with a view.

The best rooms, suites, and lanais here face out onto the private **Elbow Beach Surf Club** beach (for the exclusive use of Elbow Beach hotel guests), which is one of Bermuda's best spots to work on your tan and swim in almost completely transparent turquoise tinted waters. Although the beachfront directly in front of the hotel is reserved for hotel guests only, most visitors don't realize that there is an equally impressive public beach just next door, which shares the same exact pink sands, turquoise waters and mild waves. This is a great spot to hang out and work on your tan for a while!

Afternoon

After returning to South Road from Elbow Beach, continue along the road for another 150 meters (150 yards) and on the right side you will see the rather welcoming **Paraquet Restaurant**. This family style diner offers extremely affordable lunches and great Bermudian versions of classic comfort foods, so it is my pick for a great lunch spot.

Just about 200 meters (200 yards) further along South Road on the right side is the **Art House Gallery**. *Info*: Open from 10am until 4pm on weekdays and 10am until 1pm on high season weekends, and admission is free.

As you move east to the stop light where Middle Road and South Road merge together, you will soon pass the **Rural Hill Plaza** on the right (south) side. This quaint little shopping center is home to a **24 hour ATM** machine, the **Paget Pharmacy** which also sells sundries and newspapers, and most interesting of all, the **Ice Queen** takeout restaurant. This famous late night snack shop is open until about 5am and offers ice cream, cheap burgers and fish sandwiches, pizzas, and great French fries. This is the place that most hungry club and bar patrons mingle just after most of Hamilton's nightspots close.

A bit further east on Middle Road you will find a side street called Stowe Hill Road, which branches off to the left (north), where you'll find fine locally produced art. The **Birdsey Studio** is the best place on these islands to find original works by Bermuda's most famous scenic watercolour artist Alfred Birdsey and other members of his family. *Info*: The gallery is open from 9am until 4pm on most weekdays, and admission is free.

Continuing back along South Road you will soon have no choice but to try to navigate around the traffic circle which will shortly confront you (be extremely careful to give way to those entering before you) and instead of heading towards Hamilton, take the second exit to the left to stay on South Road as it heads westward.

About 750 meters (750 yards) further down along South Road, on the left side, is the entrance to the wonderful **Bermuda Botanical Gardens**. First opened in 1898, this dramatic collection of 36 acres of well-manicured gardens and indoor horticultural exhibits is a must-see attraction for all visitors to Bermuda. The 35-acre landscaped park contains hundreds of clearly identified flowers, shrubs and trees, including a vast collection of subtropical fruit, hibiscus, an aviary, banyan trees and a garden for the blind. *Info*: Admission to the Botanical Gardens is free from 9:30 to 3:30pm daily.

Also inside the grounds of the Botanical Gardens is fantastically beautiful official residence of the Premier of Bermuda known as **Camden**. Although used only for state functions, this early 18th century sea-view mansion is surrounded by pretty gardens and a cute fountain. A free self guided walking tour can take visitors up inside the mansion to view the fine cedar staircase and paneling, handmade cabinetry, beautiful brass and crystal chandeliers, fine period furnishings, and several portraits of former Premiers. *Info*: Open on Tuesdays and Fridays from 12noon until 2pm, and admission is free.

Free Tours of the Gardens

A great way to see the gardens might very well be to join one of the **free guided tours**. Given by several gifted and knowledgeable volunteers from the Bermuda Botanical Society, these one hour walking tours depart at 10:30am each Tuesday and Friday with occasional additional tours on Wednesdays during the high season. The guides will be glad to answer questions as they walk your group from sight to sight. Be careful not to get hit in the head by a falling scarlet cordia fruit!

Located within the Botanical Gardens is the brand new **Masterworks Museum Gallery of Bermuda Art** is worth a visit to see its collection of superb paintings by internationally recognized local and visiting artists. The world famous **Masterworks Bermudiana Collection** is comprised of paintings by internationally renowned artists like Georgia O'Keefe, Ross Turner, Albert Gleizes, Winslow Homer, who have all visited Bermuda and painted their impressions in these very canvasses. The non-profit Masterworks Foundation has tracked down these masterpieces and brought them back home to Bermuda. *Info*: The museum is open Monday through Saturday from 10am to 4pm. Admission is $5 per adult.

Evening

After heading back to your room for a shower and some well deserved rest, you may want to head into the city of Hamilton for a fine meal. I would suggest strolling along **Bermudiana Road** and see what restaurant best catches your attention. On the same street are several nice wine bars you can enjoy after dinner.

5. THE WEST END

Bermuda's northwestern most parish of **Sandys** is home to Bermuda's largest cruise ship port, several major historical sites – particularly the **Royal Naval Dockyard complex** (*seen below in the foreground*) – and a unique shopping zone. The parish is comprised of various small and large islands, including Ireland Island North, Ireland Island South, Boaz Island, Watford Island, Somerset Island, and a sliver of the western portion of Great Bermuda Island – all connected by a series of bridges.

For the most part, the rest of Sandys is fairly tranquil and residential. Boasting plenty of coastline with small but beautiful pink sand beaches, great museums, a good selection of retail shopping (even on Sundays!), superb dining and excursion possibilities, and a few great places to stay, a new and unexpected adventure seems to await visitors at the turn of each corner.

A WEEKEND ON THE WEST END

I have created **two consecutive one day tours** of the area's highlights, featuring the **Dockyard, Somerset** and **Southampton**. If venturing away from the Dockyard area, be sure to bring along a copy of the Bermuda Handy Reference Map, available for free at any Visitor's Service Bureau office, including the one at the edge of the Royal Naval Dockyard.

DAY 1
Morning
No scooter, bus or taxi is required for Day 1.

The most obvious place to start off your visit to Sandys is the **Royal Naval Dockyard,** situated directly in front of the massive new cruise ship terminal at the tip of **Ireland Island North**. Through the 1800's until 1951, when it was officially decommissioned, this was Britain's largest and most heavily fortified western Atlantic naval base of operations. Constructed primarily by thousands of ill-treated English prison convicts and slaves laboring under the direction of the British Royal Engineers, the Dockyard was designed to replace several important colonial based naval ports and repair stations on the eastern coast of what is now the United States which Britain lost use of after being defeated in the war of the American Revolution. The Dockyard

was used to launch British warships dispatched to attack Washington, DC, during the War of 1812. Countless enslaved laborers died during the dangerous conditions imposed during construction.

After several years of neglect, the Dockyard area has recently transformed into a pleasant seaside complex of boutiques, restaurants, pubs, art centers, entertainment venues, and an excellent maritime museum, all housed in a series of the naval base's original 19th century stone block buildings.

Don't Miss ...

- The Royal Naval Dockyard
- Mangrove Bay
- Somerset Bridge
- Scaur Hill Fort Park
- Cambridge Beaches
- Pompano Beach Club

This area also features great little promenades, public parks, walking trails, and comfortable benches that all face out onto the sea.

To start off your self-guided walking tour of the Dockyard area, I suggest beginning at the famed **Bermuda Maritime Museum** complex off of Maritime Lane, just a short walk away from either the public bus stop or ferry landing. This wonderful tribute to Bermuda's naval history is a must-see for all visitors. The museum is located on some ten acres of walled seaside property and is housed within a small grouping of beautifully restored stone block buildings with four foot thick walls that were originally built to house, supply, and protect British sailors that were stationed at the Dockyard.

After passing through the museum's main entrance (a stone block moated gateway through a former keep), you will be handed a small pamphlet entitled *Your Guide to the Bermuda Maritime Museum*. A self-guided walking tour of about 45 minutes will bring you through exhibits including displays of Bermudian history, British Royal Navy history, antique navigational instruments, unusual treasures discovered beneath the sea by famous local treasure hunter Teddy Tucker, whaling artifacts, antique currency, old maps, scale models of famous English sailing vessels including both the *Sea Venture* and *Deliverance*, a restored full-size Bermudian dinghy, old cannons, and lots more.

Besides these main museum buildings, visitors should also visit the former **Commissioner's House** that has finally reopened after a 20-year renovation project was recently completed. Historians believe this building to be the Western Hemisphere's first prefabricated structure (shipped over piece by piece from England in the 1820's). Another attraction on the museum's property is its series of memorable walking trials and wall walks that rise up between the bastions. If you have any specific questions about the museum, you should try to find one of the museums helpful wardens who will be happy to tell you all kinds of colorful stories and lesser-known facts. *Info*: www.bmm.bm. Tel. 441/24-1418. Admission is $10 per adult, $8 per senior citizen or students with valid ID, $5 per child less than 16 years of age, and is free for kids under five years old. A special Family Pass may be purchased for $15 that will admit two adults with up to five children. The museum's opening hours are between 9:30am and 4:30pm every day of the week.

Also located within the walls of the Maritime Museum is the new location of **Dolphin Quest**. After their success with similar adventures in both Hawaii and Polynesia, Dolphin Quest offers visitors the chance to experience a 30-minute interactive encounter in which they can stand, float or swim inside the confines of a specially redesigned salt water enclosure and touch or swim with a series of trained Atlantic bottlenose dolphins. There are several programs to choose from and they vary in length and price depending on your swimming ability, age, and budget. Prior to the actual encounter with the dolphins, participants learn basic information about these friendly creatures and their natural habitat. The experience is available to adults as well as children (at differing times), and is scheduled several times each day of the

week all year long (wet suits are both available and required during the off season due to cold sea temperatures!) rain or shine.

Also available at extra cost are behind the scenes tours, special interactivity programs, and more. Due to the often heavy demand for space for these programs during high season, reservations should be made as far in advance as possible. There are also free lectures and kids entertainment programs scheduled at least twice a week. *Info*: www.dolphinquest.org. Tel. 441/234-4464. The Dolphin Quest interactive programs currently cost between $85 and $265 per person and opening hours are between 9:30am and 5pm every day of the week. Visitor's who have paid the entrance fee to the Maritime Museum may watch the dolphins at play for free during scheduled program times.

Afternoon
As afternoon quickly approaches, it may be time to hit the beach and grab some food. Just adjacent to the museum is a small archway just off Maritime Lane leading to the tranquil **Snorkel Park Beach** and water-sports area. This small Palm lined sandy beach features a nearby offshore reef area which is quite good for snorkeling due to a large variety of colorful reef fish species as well as a sunken wreck. Boat excursions depart from here, and both snorkel and floatation gear can be rented on the premises, and admission is free of charge. The area also is home to a simple seaside restaurant called **Hammerheads Bar & Grill**, which doubles as a live music venue at least once or twice a week during the high season.

From here you can cross directly over to the other side of **Maritime Lane** and pop into the **Bermuda Arts Centre** building. This not-for-profit gallery and artists' workshops displays locally produced paintings, sculptures, jewelry, quilts, prints, photographs, and other handicrafts that are for sale in many cases. On occasion you may even find an artist hard at work creating one of a kind works. *Info*: The arts center is free to enter, and is open from 10am until 5pm every day of the week.

From the main exit door of the Arts Centre you will make a right turn to continue down Maritime Lane for a few steps until passing the arched entrance to the old **Cooperage Building**. This beautiful building was once the sight of a factory that manufactured wooden barrels that were used for storing food need on 19th century sea journeys. The majority of the Cooperage Building has now been converted to house the **Bermuda Craft Market**.

This large market is actually a collection of individual stalls that offer many items for sale including hand made Bermudian crafts, candles, quilts, stained glass, cedar wood gift items, perfumes, dolls, condiments, and other unusual items. *Info*: Admission to the craft market is free and it is open from 10am until 50pm every day of the week.

Nearby, in the inner courtyard of the Cooperage Building, is the delightful **Frog and Onion Pub** bar and restaurant that serves up some of the finest English style pub style fare in all of Bermuda. The pub's dramatic interior is embellished with stone block walls, cast iron candelabras, a massive fireplace, old billiard tables, old English public phone booths, antique portraits of sailors, and even amusing rest rooms that are known as The Poop Deck. Besides great hearty meals, the pub's long wooden and brass bar also offers a superb array of English and Bermudian beers at reasonable prices. There are also live bands that play here a couple of times each week during high season. *Info*: The pub's dining room is open from 11am until at least 9:30pm every day of the week (except during low season when it is closed on Mondays). The pub's long bar is open from 11am to 1am.

Festival Days at Dockyard

Special events such as the mid-May through mid-October **Destination Dockyard** on Monday nights from 8pm till 11pm resembles a small festival with free live music, inexpensive food kiosks, and live music & entertainment. September is the time for the Dockyard's great **Jazz Festival**, when international headliners perform live on an outdoor stage (admission to Jazz Festival is about $45 per ticket). *Info*: www.bermuda-online.org/calendar.htm.

Just across the courtyard from the pub is the main entrance to the **Neptune Cinema** where first run Hollywood movies are shown several times a day. There are also a several public bathrooms located in the Cooperage Building if needed.

After departing the Cooperage Building, make a right turn to continue heading down Maritime Lane. At the next corner you will turn right in front of the **Bone Fish Bar & Grill** and walk along a street named the **Dockyard Terrace**.

As you continue walking up the Dockyard Terrace you will pass by the **Dockyard Marina Co.** where nautical gear and great poster sized navigation charts may be purchased, and the **Dockyard Convenience Store** that sells ice-cold beverages and filling. The next important sight on this short street is the **Victualling Yard**, a fortified yard that was once the primary storage area for provisions, which were salted here and then packed into wooden barrels for use during long voyages on the open sea. This quaint targeted to be transformed into another small retail shopping and entertainment zone in order to accommodate the huge increase in cruise ship arrivals to the newly enlarged terminals here at Dockyard.

After exiting the Victualling Yard you will continue up along the Dockyard Terrace, and at the next corner bear right to wander along Maritime Lane. This long wide road is lined on the left hand side by several business including a branch of **Oleander Cycles** scooter rentals, the **Rum Cake Company** where these Bermuda rum-infused delicacies can be sampled and purchased, and the wonderful **Dockyard Glassworks** glass blowing studios and retail shop where beautiful hand made glass plates and statues can be seen (and purchased) as artisans create masterpieces of glass art in front of your very eyes. *Info*: Admission to the Glass  Blowing Studio is free and it is open from 10am until 5pm every day of the week.

After leaving the glass blowing studios, turn right and walk until the next corner when Maritime Lane merges into Camber Road. A few steps later on the right hand side you will find the **Bermuda Clay Works** pottery shop where artisans work their clay magic by hand, and a few other shops and government offices are located in converted old Naval buildings, many of which house the **Department of Marine Ports and Navigation**.

At the next corner you will keep walking straight to pass alongside the **Clocktower Centre** shopping mall. This impressive structure dates back to 1857 and was originally part of the British naval station. Set within one of the structure's two 100-foot high towers is a beautiful four-faced antique clock from London, while the other tower houses a high tide indication gauge.

You will also notice a huge sculpture in front of the main building consisting of three massive anchors that are leaning up against each other. The main Clocktower building and its adjacent west wing are surrounded by vast lawns and benches which allow visitors to sit back and ponder what the good old days must have been like for 19th century British sailors arriving on Bermuda for the first time. WEDCO – the West End Development Corp. – was responsible for developing these beautiful and rather historic buildings into the profitable shopping and recreation attraction that it has become these days, winning awards from the Bermuda National Trust for the tasteful conversion and restoration.

The lower floor of these two adjacent structures contain a variety of great boutiques, artist's studios, dining venues, and gift shops such as **Crisson's Jewelers**, **Trimminghams'** little **Trim's** shop, the **Swiss Connection** internet café, a **Makin' Waves** T-shirt shop, an **Uncommon Scents** perfume boutique, the **Ripples** kids clothing shop, **Michael Swan's** art gallery, **Calypso** and **Pier-Vu** designer women's wear stores, **Beethoven's** café and lunch spot, **A.S. Cooper &**

Segway Tours

Segway Tours Bermuda offers a delightful hour-long narrated tour of the Royal Naval Dockyard and other nearby sights at least twice a day during high season. After a short lesson in how to operate the Segway, groups of 4 to 18 participants follow behind an experienced tour director as they listen to a pre-recorded soundtrack (via headphones) explaining the unusual history of the Dockyard. *Info*: Cost is about $75 about per person. Tel. 441/504-2581. www.bermuda.com/segway.

Sons glass & porcelain emporium, **Smith's** department store, **Nannini's** Haagen Dazs ice cream parlor, the **Littlest Drawbridge** cedar wood gift shop, **Davison's** department store, **Dockyard Linens** lace and linen shop, as well as a few phone booths, public self service calling card vending machines, clean rest rooms, and ATM bank machines. *Info*: Admission to the Clocktower mall is free and it is open from 10am until 5pm every day of the week.

Evening
By now you will be fairly exhausted, so I would strongly suggest heading over to one of the Dockyards' reasonably good restaurants for your evening meal. I suggest either **Beethoven's**, **Frog & Onion pub**, **Freeport Seafood restaurant** or the **Bonefish Bar & Grill**, all located within the Dockyard zone itself.

DAY 2
Morning
Use of a public bus, taxi or scooter or taxi is required for Day 2 of this tour.

West from Dockyard to Somerset
After breakfast, depart the Royal Naval Dockyard area of Ireland Island North, and take your scooter, taxi, mini-bus shuttle, or public bus down Freeport Drive as it passes alongside the harborfront. About 700 meters (700 yards) later you will cross over **The Cut Bridge** and continue along Cockburn Road. For those interested in a nice nature park with trails and picnic areas, you can turn left onto Heydon Road and make another quick left onto Lagoon Road to reach **Lagoon Park**. This tranquil park hosts many species of birds and exotic plant life, as well as swimming areas and mangroves that can be viewed along hiking paths. Also within view are the beach area known as **Parson's Bay** and a rather photogenic inlet called **The Crawl**.

Once finished with the park and its trails, retrace your route back to Cockburn Road and continue southwest to cross over **Grey's Bridge** that leads onto **Boaz Island**. Here the road changes names again to Malabar Road before you transverse another small bridge onto **Watford Island**. The latter two islands offer little of interest to tourists other than a **ferry landing** and the adjacent small snack shop called the **Café du Quai**, but the real fun begins just after crossing the Watford Bridge onto **Somerset Island**, the largest landmass in Sandy's Parish.

Afternoon
Somerset Village & Environs
Beautiful **Somerset Island** is loaded with superb beaches, interesting attractions, nature preserves, historical sights, walking trails, cute boutiques, excellent dining possibilities in all price ranges, exciting sea-based excursions, and some of Bermuda's most intimate resorts and inns. Although most tourists don't seem to spend much time here, we strongly recommend this somewhat off the beaten path destination.

Just as you cross over the Watford Bridge, which is less than 10 minutes if coming from the Dockyard, the road changes names to

Mangrove Bay Road then passes along Somerset via the peaceful **Mangrove Bay** on your right side. When you start walking around this bay, filled with boats and featuring a fairly nice little sheltered beach area, you will see the edge of **Somerset Village** with its quaint assortment of shops and restaurants.

This area also makes a great place to stop for lunch. Both the Salt Rock Grill and the Somerset Country Squire are good afternoon meal venues and are both located right here in the village of Somerset.

In order of location on the main road at Mangrove Bay, there is a superb Sushi restaurant known as the **Salt Rock Grill**, the Bank of Bermuda's ATM machine, browse at imported sportswear at the **English Sports Shop**, check out the **W .J. Boyle & Son** shoe store, stock up on sundries at the **Somerset Pharmacy**, pick up a bottle of fine spirits at **Bud's Wine Shop**, or walk under the Moongate and relax at the bayside patio for lunch or dinner at the rather casual and moderately priced **Somerset Country Squire** restaurant and bar.

After walking, eating, and shopping your way through this part of Somerset, you have several additional possibilities for excursions, hikes, and sightseeing. A unique undersea adventure awaits all those who desire a wonderful walk on the bottom of the sea with **Hartley's Undersea Walk**. This exciting high season-only excursion puts glass bell diving helmets (big enough to wear glasses in) on both children and adults and then guides them on a spectacular walk on the shallow fish and coral dotted sea bottom. *Info*: www.hartleybermuda.com. Departures for this undersea walk take place by appointment only and leave from the backyard dock at the rustic Village Inn restaurant at the foot of the Watford Bridge (and also occasionally from Dockyard). Cost is $75.

For a nice change of pace, continue down along Mangrove Bay Road to the **Mangrove Bay Beach** area and make a right turn when you reach the area's new post office. As you wander down this small side road a small beach area will soon come into view on your right hand side. A short distance later you will turn right to soon end up at the peaceful **Mangrove Bay Wharf**. This wharf is home to the **Mangrove Marina Ltd.** excursion slips. *Info*: Tel. 441/234-0914. In high season they rent out Boston Whaler motor boats for $60 (two hours), wind-surfing boards for $15 per hour, sunfish sail boats for $20 per hour, sea kayaks for $15 per hour, and sailing lessons at $55 a person. Special sail and snorkel cruises may also be reserved with advance notice.

From the wharf you can walk or ride straight (to the west) onto Cambridge Road and then turn right (north) onto King's Point Road to reach **Cambridge Beaches**, one of Bermuda's finest and most private resorts. Although only guests are permitted to utilize Cambridge's five secluded pink sand beaches, full service spa, and two gourmet restaurants, call ahead and try to book an excellent spa treatment at its famed **Ocean Spa**.

A bit further down Cambridge Road (to the west), the street forks to both Middle Road and Daniel's Head Road. I suggest you bare right onto Daniel's Head Road for a couple of minutes until reaching the entrance for the **Somerset Long Bay Park.** This is the site of Bermuda's enchanting **Bermuda Audubon Society Nature Reserve** and has a wonderful shallow beach area. This area

is also home to **9 Beaches**, an eco-resort based around several stilted soft-sided cabanas, with sailcloth roofs, many of which jut out into the water. This fine sandy beach gets plenty of high intensity afternoon sun and is a great place to swim. The adjacent park is typically deserted except for spirited weekend family picnics where visitors are often invited to sample grandma's delicious cod fish cakes or perhaps join in a family ball game. The park is free to all visitors and is open all the time.

From the park you can continue along Daniel's Head road until turning left onto Long Bay Lane which eventually intersects with Somerset Road upon which you will turn right. About 400 meters (400 yards) later you will again turn left (east) onto Sound View Road and follow the signs to **Cavello Bay**. This is a cute little seaside residential area where time just seems to have stood still.

From the Cavello Bay Wharf you can turn right to head up along East Shore Road for 750 meters (750 yards) until reaching Somerset

Road and turn left to reach the Mangrove Bay section of Somerset Village where you will now follow Somerset Road in order to continue sightseeing around Sandys parish.

Those of you who have had enough running around can either take a ferry from the Cavello Bay Dock or Watford Bridge Dock, hop on a bus at the Somerset Bus Depot around the corner at Beacon Hill Road, call a taxi, or ride a scooter back to your hotel and save this next section of Sandys parish for yet another day.

From Somerset Village to the Bridge & Beyond
Below Somerset Village, this residential island takes on a more inactive tone. Somerset Road winds its way down the rest of this parish with the famous **Bermuda Railway Trail** running almost parallel and just about a quarter of a mile east from both this main road and most of the area's remaining attractions. Visitors to this part of Sandys and its sights can substitute the scenic Railway Trail for the more commercial Somerset Road and veer off on side streets to get to the following attractions.

From Mangrove Bay, follow Somerset Road for about 1500 meters (1500 yards) until reaching the dramatic facade and restored massive spire of the late 18th century **St. James Anglican Church**, worth a brief glimpse. As you will soon begin to notice, each parish in Bermuda has at least one Anglican (Church of England) parish church. *Info*: Open from sunrise to sunset. Fee admission.

From St. James Church, continue down Somerset Road 675 meters (675 yards) until reaching the poorly marked 44-acre **Heydon Trust Estate** on the left side of the road. The estate offers several walking paths that wind their way past fruit trees and water views. A tiny understated 17th century chapel can still be visited on the estate grounds. *Info*: Admission is free to the estate, and it is open to the public daily from 9am till 5pm.

As you continue down the road for another 85 meters (85 yards) on the left you will pass the uphill entrance to the **Scaur Hill Fort Park**. As you wander or ride up the long uphill blacktop road to the fort, the park's 22 acres of beautifully manicured grounds are a pleasant surprise. At the top of the hill visitors can tour Fort

Scaur which was a polygonal shaped moated fortress built by British Royal Engineers on the top of Somerset Island's tallest hill between 1868 and 1880 to protect the rear flank of the Royal Naval Dockyard. A self-guided tour will reveal several underground bunkers, cannons, ditches, and walls with gun slots, which where used by garrisoned British troops up to World War I and further occupied by US artillery units during World War II. The park area contains many sea view benches, and with the addition of public bathrooms has become one of the best spots in Bermuda for a romantic picnic. *Info*: Admission to the fort and park is free and it is open from 9am until 4:30pm daily.

About 1 kilometer (3/4 mile) further south on Somerset Road on the right side you will pass **Robinson's Marina** where there are several high season excursion departures. *Info*: At the marina you can rent a Boston Whaler for $45 for 2 hours, and Winner Bowriders at $65 for 2 hours from Robinson's Charter Boats, utilize the Bermuda Water-ski Center for lessons at $55 per half hour and 30 to 60 minute rides, or **Blue Water Divers scuba facilities** to take $85 beginners resort and wreck dives, $365 for a complete PADI certification course, $50 for a single tank dive, rent or purchase dive equipment and underwater cameras, and arrange all types of specialty dives and charter adventures.

Then, just a few steps past the marina, we come to the end of Somerset Island, at the foot of the world famous 17th century **Somerset Bridge**. Touted as the worlds smallest draw bridge, the bridge does not in fact open and close like a typical draw-bridge. A 32 inch wide split wooden plank can be raised from the middle of the bridge to allow the masts of Bermuda rigged sailing vessels to pass under without damage. The **Somerset Bridge Ferry Dock** at the far side of the bridge offers service back to the Royal Naval Dockyard.

After crossing over into Southampton Parish from Sandys Parish at The Somerset Bridge continue along Middle Road for another 1.4 kilometers (1400 yards) and turn right down the Pompano Beach Road. After traveling down the winding side road for 1.6 kilometers (1600 yards) you will reach clubhouse of the wonderful **Pompano Beach Club**, Bermuda's best casual seaside resort hotel (*see photo below*), sandwiched between dramatic sea cliffs and the world famous Port Royal Golf Course. Visit Pompano to take advantage of their outstanding lunch (a perfect way to unwind after a long ride to, or from, the Royal Naval Dockyard) served in the casual Oceanfront Lunch Terrace, as well as gourmet dinners available in the delightful Cedar Room and casual Ocean Grill restaurants with spectacular seaside terrace.

After visiting the Pompano Beach Club, return to Middle Road and turn right to follow it for another 1/4 kilometer (250 yards) or so before passing the entrance to the famed government owned **Port Royal Golf Course**. This dramatically landscaped 18 hole par 71 course has just undergone a massive $18 million rebuild and features 6565 yards of stunning greens and fairways and was designed by Robert Trent Jones. Known for its challenging terrain and memorable views of the sea, Port Royal is one of Bermuda's most popular places to play golf. A round here will cost around $140 per person including cart rentals (tee times should be booked well in advance by asking the front desk staff at almost any hotel on the island).

Evening
After a day like this you will need a great meal and perhaps a glass of wine to relax and enjoy. The best place to enjoy fine dining in this area are over at **Pompano Beach Club's** superb seaview **Cedar Room** and **Ocean Grill** dining rooms in neighboring Southampton parish.

6. THE EAST END

Bermuda's easternmost parish of **St. George's,** named after the patron saint of England, is steeped in history and adventure. Situated on a series of islands including **St. David's Island, St. George's Island,** and a small corner of **Great Bermuda Island,** the area was first settled when the crew of the shipwrecked *Sea Venture* landed ashore near what is now **Fort St. Catherine** on July 28, 1609.

The town of **St. George** and environs is a lot of fun. Try to spend at least a full day or even two here!

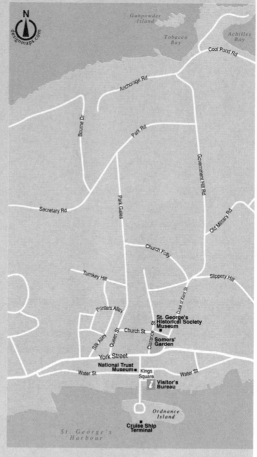

If you are visiting Bermuda during the high season, the best days to walk around this town are Monday and Tuesday when the cruise ship passengers are usually touring other parishes in the country. The feisty residents of this part of Bermuda are a bit different from most other Bermudians, especially those from the somewhat remote St. David's Island, and all have dozens of wonderful stories to tell interested visitors. If you really want to get a good feel for this parish, expect to spend at least one whole day (if not two) to explore it. Be sure to bring some comfortable shoes and a bathing suit, because you will be doing plenty of swimming and walking along the way.

A WEEKEND ON THE EAST END

Most visitors to this parish will find themselves spending much of their time walking around the city of **St. George**, so Day 1 of the tour can all be done by foot. The various church towers in the heart of the city can be seen from far away, and when cruise ships dock here they too are good landmarks to use while navigating around town. If you intend to visit more remote areas, be sure to grab a copy of the free *Bermuda Handy Reference Map*, available at any Visitor's Information Center office and which will help you avoid getting totally lost.

DAY 1
Morning
No scooter, bus or taxi is required for Day 1 of this tour.

St. George
The heart of the sleepy yet historic town of **St. George** centers on a small harbor-front plaza known as **King's Square**. The most obvious attraction here for cruise ship passengers and other tourists is the replica **Stocks & Pillory** which were once a commonly used form of punishment on the island. In the 18th and early 19th century, locals could be accused and punished for all types of offenses including swearing in public, gambling, acts of treason, robbery, murder, or even scandalous behavior. These

days the offenses are handled in a more civilized manner, although many Bermudians will privately admit that they wouldn't mind bringing back these old and rather effective deterrents. Don't be at all surprised to find young couples asking you to take their photos while they pretend to be locked up together in the stocks.

> **Don't Miss ...**
>
> • St. George
> • Tobacco Bay Beach
> • Fort St. Catherine
> • Bermuda Aquarium, Natural History Museum, & Zoo
> • Spittal Pond
> • Verdmont
> • Tucker's Town

Also in the square is the early 19th century **Town Hall** whose shuttered facade is emblazoned with a bold coat of arms. This is where the elected Mayor meets with the Corporation of St. George to discuss official business. The building's fine cedar furnishings and interior have been beautifully restored, and now include a photo gallery containing portraits of previous mayors. For those interested in a 30-minute multimedia presentation about Bermuda's history and culture, you can walk up to the top floor theater to watch the Bermuda Journey. *Info*: Town Hall is open from 9am to 4pm Monday through Saturday and admission is free. The Bermuda Journey is screened from 10am until 3pm Monday through Saturday during high season with limited showings during low season, admission is $3 for adults, $2 for seniors and children under 12.

King's Square is also surrounded by several other shops, pubs,

services, and restaurants including (starting from the southwest corner), the quaint **White Horse Tavern** restaurant and bar, a **Guerlain** perfume shop, the town's **Taxi Stand**, the **Paradise Gift Shop**, the watercolor print shop, the **Charter Bermuda** excursion and tour bookings offices, the **Bank of Bermuda**, **George & The Dragon** restaurant, and a few telephone booths. Public restrooms can be found just behind the town hall area.

As you wander around the buildings that face onto King's Square, you will find the **Bermuda National Trust Museum** (formerly the Confederate Museum). This unusual old Bermuda house, offers a permanent exhibit known as **Rogues and Runners** which offers insight into the rum runners and blockade runners that operated here during the American Revolution, the US Civil war, and the American Prohibition against alcohol. (Many Bermudians were loyal to the English crown during the colonial times as well as sympathizers to the Confederate states during these struggles). *Info*: The museum is open from 10am until 5pm Monday through Saturday during high, admission is $5 for adults, $2 for seniors and children under 12.

After finishing with the square, it's now time head south on the small bridge-road which takes you across the water and onto **Ordnance**

It's the Stocks for Ye!

During the low season on Wednesdays, an excellent **free guided walking tour**, hosted by the mayor and led by the Chamber of Commerce, starts at 10:30am from King's Square. Afterwards in the heart of the square, the oddly dressed **St. George's Town Crier** (*see photo on previous page*) stands in the middle of the square at about 12 noon and rings a bell as he shouts *Hear Ye! Hear Ye!*, and then convenes a tribunal to pronounce the sentencing of supposed criminal offenders (usually visiting tourists) to be locked into the stocks or even worse, dunked into the sea on the nearby **Dunking Stool**. Additional walking tours (without the extra added bonus of the Town Crier) are held on Wednesdays at 2pm and on Saturdays at 10:30am.

Harbour Night

On Tuesday evenings during the summer from 7pm until 10pm, St. George hosts the wonderful **Harbour Night street festivals**. This event attracts both locals and tourists of all ages who wander over towards street-side vendors selling local handicrafts, stalls offering unique foods, sidewalk fashion shows, live bands, children's activities, and extended store opening hours (some close after 9pm).

Island just in front of the cruise ship terminal. The only sight you will see here is a fairly unimpressive full size replica of the original *Deliverance*, one of two sea vessels built by the first long-term inhabitants of Bermuda, Admiral Sir George Somers and his stranded passengers and crew from the *Sea Venture*. *Deliverance II* displays reconstructions of scenes from everyday life aboard the ship and can be visited to view the living conditions that these brave venturers subjected themselves to while at sea. *Info*: The ship is open daily from 9am to 5pm. Admission is $3 per adult and $1 for kids 12 and under.

This small island has a few more points of interest including a magnificent 1.5 ton bronze statue of **Admiral Sir George Somers** by gifted local artist Desmond Fountain, whose other fine work (predominantly life-size statues of children and naked women) is prominently displayed in several galleries in the US and England, as well as other attractions and resorts in Bermuda. In the front of the island you will find a replica of the 18th century **Ducking Stool**, which was once used to dunk suspected witches and other social misfits into the cold sea. At the back of the island there is a full service passenger ship terminal that hosts large luxury liner cruise ships during the summer season.

After you are done visiting King's Square, turn right (east) at the Town Hall onto King Street. You will find a small triangle with a sculpture of famed poet Tom Moore, who resided in this town back around 1804. The building just to your left (north) is the famed **Bridge House**. Built in the early 18th century, it was once adjacent to a small bridge that carried pedestrians over a small creek which has since been land filled. In its infamous past, this was the private residence of several governors, as well as a much despised privateer Named Bridger Goodrich, who commandeered Bermudian ships trying to outrun the embargo placed on the rebellious colonies during the American Revolution. These days this fine structure still contains cedar staircases and period furnishings, but is now owned by the Bermuda National Trust and is no longer open to the public.

Continuing east to the corner of King Street and Princess Street you can see the **Old State House**. This unusual stone building was erected in 1620 for then-Governor Nathaniel Butler to host the new colony's House of Assembly, which had been meeting at St. Peter's Church but desired more privacy. The most unusual feature of this building is that of a flat roof, something you would almost never see in subsequent Bermudian structures. The building had been used by the government for quite some time, when in 1815 the capital of Bermuda was picked up and moved lock, stock, and barrel, into the city of Hamilton. The St. George Lodge of the Grand Lodge of Scotland association later acquired the right to rent this property for the sum of 1 peppercorn per year. *Info*: The building is open from 10am until 4pm on (most) Wednesdays only; admission is free.

After the State House, the road merges onto Princess Street which curves upward and intersects with King of York Street where you should cross over to wander about in **Somers' Gardens**. This peaceful garden full of palm trees and shrubs is named after Admiral George Somers. After he and his men finally departed Bermuda after being shipwrecked here on the *Sea Venture*, they arrived safely in Jamestown, Virginia. Soon after, he returned to Bermuda to pick up more supplies and check up on the few men

For Rent: 1 Peppercorn

If you are lucky enough to be in town on the closest Wednesday to April 23 each year, you are in for one of the country's most exciting events. On that Wednesday, a ceremony with much pomp and circumstance has been created for the **Grand Lodge of Scotland** to present the city of St. George with **their annual rent of 1 peppercorn**. The festivities kick off at about 11am. With the guaranteed appearance of the Governor, the Premier, the Mayor, and the Bermuda Regiment Band, the rent payment of a single peppercorn is presented to government officials upon a velvet pillow. This is one of the most spectacular old traditions still carried out in modern day Bermuda.

who had decided to stay behind on these islands. He unfortunately died in September of 1610 while on his return visit here, and his heart is said to have been buried on this spot, with the rest of his body being shipped back to England for burial. While wandering amidst the park and its collection of palm trees, shrubs, and benches, take note of the large stone memorial dedicated to this brave and honorable man. *Info*: The park is open from 8am to 4pm daily and admission is free.

After perhaps resting in the park for a while, turn back down towards town via Duke of York Street, and at the corner turn right again (north) onto Duke of Kent Street. After a block or so, you will see a set of stairs on the left (west) side of the street, just after the corner of **Featherbed Alley**, leading up to the **St. George's Historical Society Museum** and the old **Featherbed Alley Printery**. The printery contains a working model of a Gutenburg-style manual printer of the type that was once used to print the Bermuda Gazette during the the late 18th century. If the press is being utilized to print notices when you visit, ask to help in this antiquated but still effective process. *Info*: Open 10am until 4pm on Monday through Friday from April through early December.

This quaint 1730's colonial cottage has also been converted into a museum exhibiting a fine collection of early cedar furnishings, original copies of old *Bermuda Gazette* newspapers, an authentic period kitchen and pantry, a bible dating back to the mid-17th century, and lots of other local relics and artifacts. *Info*: The Museum and Printery are open 10am until 4pm on Monday through Friday from April through early November. Price is $5 per adult and $2 for kids under 12 and includes admission to both. A special combination ticket to here and several other St. George's attractions is also available.

When you're finished at the museum, continue walking up (north) on Duke of Kent Street for another block or so until seeing the haunting skeleton of the **Unfinished Church** above a hill at

the intersection before you. This half-finished Gothic church, one of my favorite spots to visit in town, was originally built in 1874 to replace St. Peter's Church. The project was abandoned midway through construction due to a combination of funding problems, a roof collapse, and various political reasons.

These days a team of builders and landscapers can be seen occasionally renovating and strengthening the structure, which was turned over to the Bermuda National Trust. Some say that it may actually be re-roofed one day. The church is not open to the public due to safety concerns, but you can still see much of its barren interior, supporting buttresses, and facade from street level.

Once you've taken a few good pictures of the church, retrace your steps back down (south) on Duke of Kent Street, passing again by the Historical Society, and then immediately turning right (west) onto Featherbed Alley.

At the next corner you will keep going straight (west) onto Church Lane. You should then make your first right (north) turn onto Broad Alley to find the **Old Rectory House**. This quaint small house, built in the 17th century by a retired pirate, is now owned by the Bermuda National Trust. During the early 18th century the house was occupied by Reverend Alexander Richardson of St. Peter's Church, hence the name Old Rectory. You can get an interesting glimpse into the life of Rev. Richardson from several antiques and personal effects which are on display. *Info*: The house is open on Wednesdays only, from 10am until 5pm, and admission is free.

From the Old Rectory follow No Name Lane until the next corner where you will turn left onto Queen Street and stop in at the **Bermuda Perfumery** to smell the floral scents made here in Bermuda. *Info*: The perfumery is open Monday through Saturday from 10am until 5pm, and admission is free.

Continue on Queen Street downhill until the next intersection where you will turn left (east) onto Duke of York Street. About half-way down the block, you can't help but be drawn to the fantastic whitewashed facade and portal of **St. Peter's Church**. This beautiful Anglican Church was originally erected in 1619 on the spot of a wooden thatched roof structure that dated back to 1612. After in-curring severe hurri-cane damage, the church had to be com-pletely rebuilt in 1713, with the side wings and clocktower being added in the early 19th century to accommodate a growing congregation. During the course of these construction projects, the church's original cedar altar and some old cedar pews were salvaged and are still in use.

The church's great vestry contains a collection of old Bermudian coins, and 17th century Royal English silver communion sets and chalices that should also be seen. In 1620, Bermuda's first House of Assembly session took place here. While visiting the church, make sure to take a good look at the unusual memorial plaques that line many of the interior walls. Behind the church is a peaceful graveyard that can be visited to see the inscribed grave- stones of many people including assassinated Governor Sir Rich- ard Sharples, and American sailor Richard Dale who lost his life during the War of 1812 (St. George was a hotbed of British military activity before the naval attack on America). *Info*: The church is open daily from 9am until 4:30pm and admission is free.

Afternoon
Since there are many fine shops and eating establishments along the path to your next few in-town attractions, I suggest returning to King's Square for a cold drink or a snack. For the best afford- able cuisine in town I would suggest either **The White Horse Tavern** or **Café Gio,** both off Water Street.

After you have regained both your strength, turn left (west) onto **Water Street** and do a little well deserved window shopping. Keep your eyes out for the 24 hour **ATM** bank machine, English and American shoes at **W.J. Boyle & Sons**, fine women's swimwear and fashion clothing at **Frangiapani**, fine imported jewelry and watches at **Crisson's**, a vast assortment of gifts and men's and women's clothing at the **Making Waves**, and the old **St. George's Post Office** which dates back to about 1760. Also look out for **E.R. Aubrey** jewels, the fine **The Carriage House** restaurant, **The Book Cellar**, a **Vera P Card** giftshop featuring watches and fine china, and a **Crown Colony** ladies resort wear outlet and the superb **Carriage House** restaurant.

Next you will pass a quaint harbor front shopping mall called the **Somers Wharf**. In this center you will find the **A. S. Cooper &**

Sons china, crystal, and perfume shop, **Davison's** T-shirt shop, a branch of **The Island Shop** know for its decorative arts, and the **English Sports Shop** with its fine selection of imported gents sportswear, the **Crown Colony** ladies clothing shop, and finally the **Tavern by the Sea** restaurant that features live music on many evenings. This water view strip of wharfs and moorings leads past the outdoor tables of various eating establishments, and heads westward towards the other cruise ship terminal.

If you retrace your steps back up to **Water Street** and turn left (west) at the Carriage Museum, on the opposite side of the street you will find the entrance to the **Tucker House**. Originally built on what was then the town's waterfront in 1711, this limestone house was later home to the infamous Tucker family.

This politically connected family was caught up in a legendary plot that still provokes anger in some Bermudians. When the American colonies decided to revolt against Mother England, the revolutionary Colonial Congress imposed an export embargo on all British colonies that did not support their struggle. Since the vast majority of Bermudians were rather loyal to the crown, they were subject to a cut-off of badly needed food supplies from America. Under cover of darkness, a group of men, including a couple of the Tuckers, stole several dozen kegs of gunpowder from the local arsenal on August 14, 1775, and loaded them onto ships in nearby Tobacco Bay, which were headed for Boston. The result was that food supplies were kept flowing to Bermuda throughout the duration of the supposed embargo.

The house, now owned by the Bermuda National Trust, contains a number of 18th century English mahogany and Bermudian cedar furnishings, oil paintings of prominent Tuckers, crystal chandeliers, fine engraved silver, and other family heirlooms. Downstairs, in what was once the kitchen is an exhibit dedicated to local barber Joseph Hailey Rainey, a former slave who escaped to Bermuda during the Civil War. He would later return to the south after the war, and was eventually elected as the first black Congressman in the United States. *Info*: Open 10am until 4pm on Monday through Saturday. Admission is $5 per person.

As Water Street keeps heading west, you will also pass by the **Caffe Latte's Cyber Café** and just next door is the **Visitors Information Center** office where you can pick up free maps and brochures to local attractions. They can also be quite helpful with restaurant recommendations and directions for the utterly lost. *Info*: The bureau is open from 9am until 1pm and from 2pm until 4:30pm Monday through Saturday during high season, and is closed on most days during the low season.

There is not much left to see on Water Street other than **St. George's Cycle Livery** scooter and moped rental shop, and a few other new shops.

Now that you have seen just about all the major sights in the town of St. George, just keep walking up the street for another block or so as it changes its name to Blacksmiths Hill Road and turn right to head back to **Duke of York Street** to hit the rest of the shops and unusual venues.

The Outskirts of St. George
After checking out the town of St. George for several hours, you can now see the many other dramatic sights of this special parish. From the town, you can take buses, taxis, scooters, or enjoy a brisk 15 minute hike between town and most of the following attractions.

First stop is **Tobacco Bay Beach**, which is about 875 yards hike or ride from King's Square. From the heart of town follow **Duke of Kent Street** uphill all the way north (out of town) until it dead ends at the Un-finished Church. At the dead-end in front of the Church you will bear right and fol-low the road up-hill for 100 yards or so until reach-ing an unnamed lane that passes through the golf

golf course area. This scenic lane then merges onto **Barry Road** which borders the tip of this peninsula, and you will soon end up directly in front of a sheltered sandy cove known as Tobacco Bay Beach. Here you can swim up to naturally formed sea arches and boulders in perfect safety from the current. During the summer, the beach is full of ghost-white passengers just arriving in town from the cruise ships that dock nearby, but if you get here early enough, it is a fantastic place to relax. A few small beachfront buildings will rent snorkeling gear and flotation devices by the hour in high season, as well as selling hot dogs, hamburgers, French fries, tuna sandwiches, grilled cheese, and cold sodas. Public restrooms and changing facilities are also available. The beach is open from sunrise to sunset, and admission is free.

From Tobacco Beach, head along Barry Road for another 450 yards until reaching the most breathtaking fortress which can be seen in Bermuda, **Fort St. Catherine** (*see photo on page 62*). Built on the site of an older fortification dating back to 1614, this massive restored defensive fort was actually rebuilt and expanded in the 19th century, and was the area's first line of defense against the incursion of American warships during the war of 1812. With it high position above the bluffs where many of the *Sea Venture* crewmen first reached Bermuda after their shipwreck, the fort must have been an awesome deterrent.

After crossing over the moat to enter the fort, you will be taken on a self guided subterranean tour which leads past several scale model reconstructions of scenes starting from the initial wreck of the *Sea Venture*, and continuing through the launch of the *Deliverance*, the repulsion of Spanish invaders in the 1600's, English sponsored privateering and local pirate activity, use of the Dunking Stool for punishment, and the theft of local gunpowder for the American revolutionaries. Next you will descend down into the tunnels that were cut right into the bedrock, and enter the basement. You will first pass by displays of old uniforms, armaments, and lanterns until you have reached the first of several cubby hole sized exhibits with mannequins dressed in 19th century uniforms and recorded announcements. After viewing the magazines used to store the 181 kilogram (400 pound) loaded shells and the hand operated shell elevators, you will be led to a large room containing a fantastic collection of antique swords and rifles.

Now you are brought back up to the ground floor. Here you will walk past several cannons to enter the keep with its stairs and tunnels leading to the kitchen area, and finally reach the former gun room which now is used to display a replica collection of England's Crown Jewels, gem encrusted swords, orbs, scepters, and other royal relics. As you exit through the rooftop, keep your eyes out for the huge English built 10" muzzle loaded guns that face the sea.

George the Ghost

While you are wandering through the fort, you will most certainly find out about the fort's most famous fromer inhabitant, **George the Ghost**. Although it may not seem that scary to you, enough respectable people experienced a spirit or strange noises firsthand in these tunnels that in 1978 the church performed an exorcism to remove any ghosts or evil spirits. Since then, only the electronic version of George has been confronting visitors.

Info: The fort complex is open daily from 10am until 4pm. Admission is $5 per adult and $2 for kids under 12 when accompanied by an adult.

Adjacent to the fort is a beach simply known as **Fort. St. Catherine Beach** which is home to the **Beach It** seaside water sports center where you can rent boats, jet skis, and snorkel gear or just enjoy a cold cocktail and a simple lunch while working on your tan. This area was formerly the sight of a Club Med hotel which is soon to be the new sight of a Park Hyatt resort. The area was also home to the Robert Trent Jones-designed **St. George's Golf Course**. This is an 18 hole par 62 oceanside course of 4043 yards.

Another 1200 yards or so further along Barry Road, as it continues to trace the peninsula's windswept coastline, you will come to a 19th century rectangular fortification known as the **Alexandra Battery**. Its three massive guns were used to defend the St. George's area from intruders off the coast, and can still be visited to climb to its turret. *Info*: The battery is open from 10am until 4pm daily, and admission is free. Almost adjacent to the battery, the first of several bays and beaches that you will now pass is known as **Building's Bay**. Besides possibly being the settlement sight of the stranded crew from the Sea Venture, it was also where the crew built one of the ships which would later take them safely, but not in comfort, to Jamestown. The bay and its beach are open from sunrise to sunset, and admission is free, but don't expect any public restrooms or other facilities.

A mere 150 yards away from the Battery is the smaller **Gates Fort**. The restored limestone block structure was one of Bermuda's first defensive fortress. It was probably built around 1622 and is named after Sir Thomas Gates, one of the Sea Venture crewmen who first came ashore on this spot. He was later to become colonial Jamestown, Virginia's Governor. Since the fort later was converted into a private residence, a restoration was necessary to recreate its original ambiance. The views are rather impressive. The fort is always open and admission is free.

From here you can return to town retracing your steps to Tobacco Bay along Barry Road, and turning up onto Naval Tanks Hill which will take you back through the golf course area and lead you to Duke of Kent Street and then back into the heart of town.

Evening
After leaving the beaches of this area, have a great (and afford-able) dinner on the harbour-view patio of the laid-back **Tavern by the Sea**, or the more opulent **Carriage House**. After that head over to one of the few pubs in King's Square as there is simply no other nightlife options in this tiny town!

DAY 2
Morning
Use of a Public Bus, taxi or rental scooter is required for this day of the tour.

Shelly Bay & Flatts
From St. George, follow Duke of York Street eastward out of town, as it first merges with Mullet Bay Road and then bear right onto **Kindley Field Road** which passes along the airport and then leads to the causeway's bridge.

After crossing the bridge, bear right onto Blue Hill Road which soon leads onto **North Shore Road**. In about 3 kilometers (2 miles) you will reach beautiful **Shelly Bay Beach**. This beautiful wide sandy roadside beach has an unusually calm and shallow basin where you can walk out in waist deep water to cool off or even fish. Since this is one of the few beaches along the northern coast, it is seldom crowded, has lots of trees to sit under, and has several facilities including a beach house with public restrooms, exceedingly cold showers, high season snack bar and snorkel equipment rental shop, and its own bus stop. Nearby is the small but peaceful mangrove-filled **Shelly Bay Park and Nature Reserve** where you can hike about or relax and enjoy a scenic picnic on one of the wooden tables. *Info*: The beach and park are both always open, and admission is free.

After about 2.25 kilometers (2 miles) or so further along North Shore Road, you will see the entrance to the **Bermuda Aquarium, Natural History Museum, and Zoo**, which besides the beaches has become Bermuda's top tourist attraction. Founded in 1942, this large complex has recently been able to acquire an additional $1.5 million to renovate and expand the facilities, which attract over 120,000 visitors yearly. Presently, the complex offers a wide range of exciting exhibits which should be seen by all visitors to the nation.

Upon entry, you will first find yourself inside the two-room indoor **Bermuda Aquarium** wing with its 26 tanks filled with unfiltered seawater from Harrington Sound. Make sure to pick up one of the complimentary audio wands which will help guide you past the various tanks containing spiny lobsters, tilefish, groupers, moray eels, sergeant major fish, sea anemone, blue angle fish, parrotfish, bream, squirrelfish, squid

flounder,   pudding wife, jewelfish, and sardines who are kept under conditions that, although somewhat cramped, tend to mimic their natural environment.

After passing by the outdoor harbor seal pools, you will be led inside the **Bermuda Natural History Museum**. This part of the complex was designed as an entertaining and educationally motivated collection of local geology, ecology, and scientific exhibits that are all rather well explained. You will find well presented photos, maps, and diagrammatic explanations about the islands' volcanic origins, indigenous plant and tree life, migratory birds, ocean currents, climate, caves, seacoast, and interior lands. One of the more unusual items on display is the documentation and 2-ton circular **Bathysphere** used by New York Zoological Society's Dr. William Beebe in 1930 to dive a record 3,028 feet off the coast of Bermuda. Also at the exit of this building you can take a quick look at all of the world's record game fish catches caught off Bermuda.

After leaving the museum, you will then pass by a series of outdoor cages, aviaries, ponds, and pens that comprise the **Bermuda Zoo**. Some of the inhabitants include otters, two toed sloths, golden lion tamarins, barn owls, ducks, flamingos, alligators, iguanas, tortoises, and a couple of bizarre animals such as Malayan water monitors and Madagascar ringtail lemurs. The complex also contains a summertime children's petting zoo, an interactive audio-visual enhanced invertebrate house, a wildlife rehabilitation center for sick and injured wildlife and birds, a weekend student Discovery Room and teaching program, public restrooms, and a nice little gift shop. *Info*: 40 North Shore Road. www.bamz.org. Tel. 441/293-2727. Admission here is valid for all wings and exhibits throughout the complex. Also note that you can watch the seals being feed daily at 9am, 1:30pm and 4pm.The doors are open from 9am until 4pm daily, admission is $10 per adult, $5 per senior citizens, $5 per child under 13, and free for kids under 5.

Afternoon
Harrington Sound, Spittal Pond, Mansions & Caves
From the Aquarium and Zoo you are just steps away from a bridge leading across **Flatts Inlet**. This inlet is the primary source

of the saltwater and aquatic life that fills the adjacent **Harrington Sound**, and also is the main point of access for local boats to reach the open sea. In the old days of privateers and pirates, the most successful  smugglers would unload their cargo here under a vail of darkness to avoid being searched by customs officials. These days, this side of the inlet is surrounded by a series of multimillion dollar waterside condominiums with their own yacht moorings and docks. The tiny adjacent hamlet of **Flatts** is worth a few minutes of time to explore, and has a nice restaurant called **Rustico's** which is a good place to stop and enjoy a pasta and pizza for lunch.

At this point you have found yourself at one of the busiest intersections in this end of the country. Be patient here to avoid accidents, especially during rush hours when these roads get quite busy. Here you will find a small pink cottage, which is the office of **Bermuda Bell Diving**. Without the slightest doubt, this is Bermuda's most unusual and compelling sea excursion. They run a three hour excursion aboard a 40' motor yacht with a special twist. This amazing trip climaxes with a 30-minute guided walk on the sea bottom during which clients wear large brass helmets (big enough to wear glasses under) and can actually reach out and touch the fish and sea anemones near several coral reef areas. *Info*: Tel. 441/535-8707. They have both morning and afternoon departures (high season only), and this worthwhile adventure only costs about $70 per person. They also can arrange for a St. George pick-up for cruise ship passengers.

From Flatts village, turn onto **Harrington Sound Road** and then after about 500 meters (500 yards) bear right onto **Harrington Hundreds Road** and then after another 1.3 kilometers (1 mile) bear right onto **South Road** heading southwest. The next interesting spot to pop into along the way is the **Harrington Hundreds Grocery** on the right side of South Road. This is certainly the best major grocery store in all of Bermuda and it is where you can buy the finest imported gourmet foods and picnic supplies. Even if you are staying all the way on the other side of the country, I still suggest doing some of your grocery shopping here.

Continuing southwestward along South Road you will soon pass the next attraction which is **Spittal Pond Nature Reserve**. The

park's Spittal Pond (now partially fenced in to protect the birds) is the heart of a 59 acre wildlife sanctuary that is managed by the Bermuda National Trust. This nature preserve, the largest in all of Bermuda, is home to hundreds of different lizards, crab, and bird species. There are a number of different trails that start at the reserve's east and west parking lots and head past the pond. If you visit here during the off season, you stand an excellent chance of seeing hundreds of migratory birds without binoculars. The impressive nature trails then take you past cactus-filled coastal lookouts and towards the strange **Checker Board** of giant rectangular geological formations at land's end. Although at first it may seem a bit bizarre, this is the most magical spot in the whole country, and has captivated me for hours at a time.

Continue wandering down the poorly marked trails and you'll pass desolate sea cliffs with Longtail nesting sites, scary open caves, and onward to the so-called **Spanish Rock**. This large boulder stands on a bluff overlooking the sea and carries an inscription containing a cross with the initials R.P. and the date of 1543. Although the rock was initially thought to have been carved on by Spanish sailors (hence the name Spanish Rock), most historians now believe that this was the work of shipwrecked Portuguese sailors. After decades of locals and tourists carving their own initials next to the original inscription, and the heavy erosion caused by the constant spray of sea water, the ancient cipher was replaced by a bronze replica. Unfortunately, some of the less intelligent visitors to this area have since started carving their own messages into the bronze plaque. While walking through the reserve, please keep on the trails as not to disturb the somewhat nervous wildlife in the area. *Info*: The reserve and its trails are open daily from sunrise to sunset and admission is free.

Return to **South Road** and continue to follow it southwestward for about another 1.25 kilometers (1 mile) or so until turning right down a small lane called **Collectors Hill Road**, follow it to the very top until seeing the signs marking the entrance to **Verdmont**. This beautiful Georgian-style hilltop mansion dates back to 1710, and contains a large collection of antique period furnishings that have been assembled by the Bermuda National Trust.

When you visit this fine example of early 18th century architecture, make sure to spend some time seeing each of the eight fireplace-filled rooms on its two charming floors and upstairs attic that are all connected by a fine cedar staircase. The first floor contains a Parlour Room with 18th century Bermudian cedar cabinetry and an English piano from the same period, the Drawing Room has 18th and 19th century portraits of former residents (the Smith Family) originally lit by the various hurricane candle shades like the ones on display, and a vast Dining Room featuring an early 18th century Bermudian gateleg table and cedar Wainscot chairs. The second floor can be visited to see the two bedrooms containing four poster cedar beds and cedar highboy chairs, as well a secondary Parlour which exhibits a fine Chippendale cabinet and side chairs along with fine 18th century Chinese porcelain, and a French blue and gold tea set said to have been captured by local pirates while en route to America in 1815. The third floor attic nursery contains an unusual assortment of curiosities including children's toys and an old rocking horse.

Since many of the items are not marked with descriptive tags, be sure to ask for a free copy of the Verdmont Historic House pamphlet which details the stories of the unusual antiques, residents, and history of this fine estate. *Info*: Tel. 441/236-7369. The mansion is open from 10am until 4pm from Tuesday through Saturday, and admission costs $5 per adult, $2 for ages 6-18.

After leaving Verdmont, retrace your long route back up to **Harrington Sound Road**, and this time turn right to follow alongside the Harrington Sound itself. After several kilometers the road merges with Wilkinson Ave, at which point you should keep your eyes out for signs for **Crystal & Fantasy Caves**. About 750 meters (750 yards) down Wilkinson Ave. on the left side you will find a well-marked turnoff that eventually leads to both the **Crystal Caves** and the **Fantasy Caves**, which are adjacent to one another.

These are the most impressive of the area's many caves and were first discovered by a pair of boys chasing a runaway ball down a small hole in the ground. The hole was soon excavated to uncover a massive cavern over 100 feet below surface level. The caves include an underground salt water ocean feed lake that rises and falls with the tides and can reach up to 18 meters (54 feet) in depth. The cave's top and bottom of the caves are covered by limestone stalagmites and stalactites forming unusual patterns, including

what the guides point out as the Manhattan skyline. It's important to remember that these giant formations are naturally created at the rate of only 1 cubic inch per 100 years. Guided tours are given by shouting staff members who lead you down a long slippery staircase and onto a series of floating bridges. Don't touch the formations, or else you will be in violation of the law! *Info*: www.caves.bm. Tel. 441/293-0640. The caves are open from 9:30am until 4:30pm (last tour at 4pm) daily, except for low season when it may close on Mondays and for the whole month of January. The required group tours depart about every 30 minutes throughout the day. Admission is $14 per adult, $8 for kids 5-12, and free for children under 4.

Evening
Since you are already all the way out near the caves and Blue Hole Hill, I strongly suggest one of 2 options in the area. Near the caves is a superb fine dining establishment known as **Tom Moore's Tavern** which is among the best restaurants in eastern Bermuda.

If a formal expensive meal is not on your agenda tonight, another extremely memorable place to eat (and drink!) would be over at the infamous **Swizzle Inn** pub and restaurant on Blue Hill Road, which you will pass on the way back to St. George. Located about half a kilometer (500 yards) or so south of the causeway leading to the airport, make sure to try their amazing Rum Swizzle, but be careful as these pack a strong punch!

DAY 3
Morning
Use of a taxi or rental scooter is required for Day 2 of this tour.

From the town center, follow **Duke of York Street** out of town to the east, as it merges with Mullet Bay Road. Now you can stop at a couple of fine seaside parks with benches and trails including Mullet Bay Park and Rocky Hill Park. A few hundred meters (yards) ahead, bear right onto **Ferry Road**.

This street will lead past a few oil tanks, and into the 22 acre **Ferry Point Park**. While in the park you can visit a couple of old cemeteries and ruined fortresses, swim, fish, picnic, and visit the **Martello Tower**. Built in 1823 to support a huge gun that could swivel to any direction needed, the tower now offers visitors a great panoramic lookout point over much of the northern coastline.

Now you should head back in the direction of the bridge that crosses over Ferry Point, but do not yet cross it. Instead, keep your eyes out for **Biological Lane** and the signs leading to the **Bermuda Institute of Ocean Sciences**, which really should be experienced before departing the island. Founded in 1926, this world class scientific facility is operated as an American non-profit research organization, hosting leading scientists from all over the globe. Besides containing a vast library of science and marine biology materials, the station offers a slew of courses, seminars, whale watching excursions, work study programs, and marine education camps to advanced international students, as well as an Elderhostel program for more mature groups.

The station operates dozens of state of the art laboratories, a seagoing research vessel, a remote controlled underwater video hydrobot robot, and an on-line Internet link to the rest of the world. Among the recent research conducted here are studies on subjects ranging on the long-term effects of oil spills on tropical marine ecosystems, to the satellite analysis of ocean biogeochemistry. *Info*: www.bios.edu. Tel. 441/297-1880. The station is open to the public on Wednesdays, when they offer a free tour with refreshments starting at 10am.

St. David's Island
From St. George's Island, cross over the bridge that leads over **Ferry Reach** and take the traffic circle to the 3rd turnoff to reach **Swalwell Drive**, which heads east alongside the runways of the International Airport. You are actually on a landfill of three smaller islands joined together to form what is now known as **St. David's Island**.

This is a rather unusual island, with many of its residents voluntarily isolating themselves from the rest of the country. They even speak with their own sort of accent here. In fact, many of these humble and hard working locals are the descendants of American Indians who were brought to Bermuda as manual laborers. Much of the island is strictly off limits to the general public, as it contains NASA space tracking stations (and the facilities of the former **US Naval Air Station** complex).

Swalwell Drive will go through several name changes and bends during the approximately 4 kilometer (4000 yards) run before finally reaching the intersection of **Texas Road** where you will be turning right (south). This small street eventually leads to the foot of the **St. David's Lighthouse.** This stone block lighthouse dates back to 1879, and can be climbed to enjoy magnificent views from its panoramic balcony. *Info*: The lighthouse is open daily from May through October only, and admission is free.

Afternoon
St. David's & Tucker's Town
If you are hungry, return to the main road and look across the way to the waterfront. This is where you will find the **Black Horse Tavern**, a casual affordable local restaurant with great local seafood and massive burger specials.

From the tavern, turn right (east) and continue on the main road until you are able to turn right (southeast) onto **Battery Road**. Soon you will be entering into **Great Head National Park**, which among other things is the official finish line for the world famous yearly Newport, Rhode Island to Bermuda yacht race.

The park also contains **St. David's Battery**, which was built in the 1800's to house and protect 4 British made 6" and 9.2" guns that could propel shells upwards of 33 kilometers (20 miles) out to sea. *Info*: The park and its fort can be visited from 10am until 4pm daily, admission is free.

If you head back to the main road, and follow it to the very end, it will merge with a small street called Cashew City Road that leads to an interesting area that resembles a remote Louisiana Bayou (or perhaps a scene from the film Deliverance) called **Little Head Park**. The park itself is just a place for boats to moor, but one of the small wooden buildings next to it is home to **Dennis's Hideaway**, the most authentic old school Bermudian restaurant in existence. Sea Leg Lamb, the restaurant's owner, serves up old Bermudian seafood recipes like shark hash and mussel chowder. Don't expect opulence here because dining in this place is more like being invited into someone's rural living room for a meal.

Before retracing your route back towards the Airport, if you are here on a Wednesday, call 297-1376 and ask see the **Carter House**. Once inside, you can view the 17th century house built in 1640 of limestone and cedar by the son of Christopher Carter, a Sea

Venture crewman who decided to stay behind after the rest of the crew sailed onward to Jamestown. The house is now used as a museum for Bermudian culture and US military history. *Info*: The museum is open from 11am until 3pm on Wednesdays only, and admission is free.

Tucker's Town

After leaving St. David's Island via the **Long Bird Bridge** and its adjacent causeway, continue to the end of **Blue Hole Hill Road**, and turn left (south) onto **Harrington Sound Road**. After passing the entrance to **Castle Harbour**, bear left onto **Paynter's Road** and take it for about 1 kilometer (1000 yards) until reaching the intersection of South Road where you will turn left (east). The lush green landscaping that you will now see is actually the beginning of the most exclusive residential area in all of Bermuda, **Tucker's Town**.

This rather private suburb, with its multimillion dollar estates and now even timeshare apartments are all owned by American, European, and Bermudian millionaires who all seem to guard their privacy in a serious way. The area consists of a few small and winding lanes that have magnificent estates hidden on private access roads, many of which face the sea. The most notorious home owner here is H. Ross Perot, who reportedly dynamited the reef in front of his sea-view estate when local authorities refused to give him permission to expand his boat dock. As long as you don't trespass onto private property, you can still do a fair amount of mansion viewing from the side of several small roads that divide the area.

More Beaches & Golf

From here the **Tucker's Town Road** veers off to the right at just about the point where South Road ends. Nearby is a side road leading to the brand new luxury resort (not completed at press time) called the **Tucker's Point Hotel & Spa** which also has a nearby golf course.

Take the right turnoff to continue following Tucker's Town Road for another 250 yards and turn right just down a small road just before reaching a security gatehouse which usually stops all traffic from continuing (except for residents of the further reaches of this private road). From the turnoff just before the gatehouse, go straight for a short distance until turning left on another small lane, which will bring you to the **Natural Arches** beach with its unusual rock formations.

The nearby private **Mid Ocean Club Golf Course** is still Bermuda's most exclusive private course. With its fine 18 hole par 71 championship course of 6547 yards, this is the site of several PGA-sanctioned tournaments each year. This is a private club, and either your hotel's concierge (if they have the right connections) or a club member may be needed to get you a tee off time here. The club also sports a fine Clubhouse restaurant, two tennis courts, private beaches, and 20 terraced rooms that are only available to guests. In any case, the non-member price for these fine links is about $150 per round.

Evening
Try the Tucker's Point Hotel's pricey but excellent restaurants (already open for business) including the **Grille Terrace**, **Golf Clubhouse** and the **Beach Club**. Proper attire and reservations are required. If this is out of the question due to price or dress code or lack of availability, head back to the town of St. George and try one of the pubs for dinner (see the *Best Sleeps & Eats* chapter).

7. ONE WEEK IN BERMUDA

Most visitors to Bermuda book a vacation for one week or so in duration. The following condensed 7-day itinerary combines the best of Bermuda's beaches, historic sights, gardens, parks, fortresses, shopping districts and unique restaurants. All of the sights selected for this weeklong tour can be accessed via a short walk from a regularly scheduled public bus and/or ferry route(s), followed by a short walk. See the previous destination chapters for specifics about the destinations listed in this chapter.

Feel free to switch which days you decide to devote to these specific set of activities, as weather should be a major determining factor in your daily schedule!

DAY 1
The South Shore Beaches

Since the beaches here are perhaps the islands' top attractions, I would suggest starting out on Bermuda's famous South Shore coastline just after enjoying a hearty breakfast.

A perfect day of sun & sand would start at **Horseshoe Bay Beach**. Blessed with silky soft pink sands and dramatic rocky cliffs, this is a great place to spend at least half a day. There are plenty of on-sight services here (including a snack shop, public restrooms & changing facilities) plus there are many smaller and less crowded cove beaches all along the adjacent **South Shore Park** area, all of which are easily accessible from Horseshoe Bay via a series of footpaths.

As the midday sun starts to become too hot to handle, an extended lunch-break along with some ice cold beverages of your choice may be in order. Although the snack shop at Horseshoe Bay Beach is fine for hot dogs and cold sandwiches, two better bets are just a few minutes ride away. I would strongly suggest that if you are looking for a casual restaurant with a much more substantial menu and great cocktails, head over to **The Swizzle** on South Road.

Although there are many other fine beaches in the area, my choice for the perfect spot to enjoy your afternoon sunbathing and swimming would be over at **Elbow Beach** *(see photo on previous page)*. Although the beach area directly in front of the resort hotel is officially reserved for hotel guests, and equally impressive public beach is situated just a couple of minutes walk along the sand to the west. This is also great place to swim as combination of turquoise waters and pink sand is simply awesome.

For a superb seaside dinner, try **Mickey's** or the more formal **Restaurant Lido** located on the Elbow Beach Hotel's sea-side terrace. Both of these restaurants offer impressive Italian influenced cuisine served up with sunset views that will take your breath away.

DAY 2
The Capital City of Hamilton

Bermuda's exciting little capital city of **Hamilton** deserves to be visited on several occasions during a week to Bermuda. Besides offering a wide variety of duty-free shopping and esoteric dining possibilities, it is well worth the effort to make your way into town for special events such as each Wednesday evening's **Harbour Nights**. This is also the place to best enjoy a memorable pub crawl and the experience island nightlife, especially on Friday nights when the well heeled after work crowd spills into the best pubs & wine bars.

A perfect day in Hamilton would start off shortly after breakfast along historic **Front Street**, where you can shop at over three dozen superb designer boutiques. From inexpensive T-Shirts and Postcards to opulent luxury goods such as Swiss watches and Italian shoes, Front Street has the full range covered. A short walk around **Queen Street** and **Reid Street** will take you to where the locals and reinsurance company employees hunt for bargains.

Also whilst downtown, be sure to check out **Par-La-Ville Park**. This wonderful palm and shrub-filled Public Park filled with manicured gardens of exotic plants and trees. Just next door is the **Perot Post Office**, Bermuda's first official post office which opened in 1848.

By now you may want to grab a bite for lunch, and while in town, I strongly suggest you head for either **The Lemon Tree Cafe** on Queen Street, **La Baguette** on Burnaby Street, or the **Paradiso Café** on Reid Street.

From here it is a brisk 15-minute walk to the east edge of town and onto Happy Valley Road, until reaching Fort Hamilton Drive which leads directly to **Fort Hamilton**. This is a picturesque spot that is perfect for panoramic views over the downtown and harbour. This 19th century fort offers a chance to explore its fortifications, shrub filled moats, stone tunnels, and gun placements, all for free!

As dinnertime approaches, there are many good choices for Bermudian & International cuisine in town. Among my personal favourites in the downtown core is the Sushi bar at the **Harbourfront** at B.U.E.I. and the Arabesque **Café Cairo** or Thai styled **Silk**, both on Front Street. If you don't mind a 15 minute walk to the west (or a 3 minute taxi or scooter ride) make it a point to call **Ascots** and book a table for a sumptuous and romantic culinary experience.

After dinner you can visit several bars and pubs and wine bars to find the perfect spot for an after dinner cocktail. Most of the nightlife takes place along Front Street and Bermudiana Road. Try checking out the **Pickled Onion, Flanagan's, Robin Hood Pub,** the **Hog Penny** and **Café Cairo** for the most action.

DAY 3
The Dockyard & West End
I suggest a more calm and relaxing schedule today. Throughout Bermuda there are many small ports that offer direct and/or non-stop ferry service to major destinations including the Royal Naval dockyard. The ferry is a great way to relax and see the views, meet the locals and of course avoid all the rush hour traffic on the roads.

Upon arrival at the **Royal Naval Dockyard** ferry pier, head straight for the nearby info center of **Segway Tours Bermuda** and take a rather pleasurable hour long narrated motorized Segway tour of the entire Dockyard zone. After a few minutes of instruction on how to use these unique 2 wheeled personal transporters, you will have a blast rolling along the area's lanes and side streets.

From here it is just a short walk away to the impressive **Bermuda Maritime Museum** complex off of Maritime Lane, where you will find exhibitions about Bermuda's naval history. Admission to the beautiful **Commissioner's House is** also included. The **Dolphin Quest** staging area is just next door for those who were lucky enough to have pre-booked reservations to swim with the dolphins.

Just steps away you can visit the **Bermuda Arts Centre** which displays locally produced paintings, sculptures, jewellery, quilts, prints and photographs, while next door you can purchase Bermudian made crafts and food products at **Bermuda Craft Market** and sample tasty treats at the nearby **Bermuda Rum Cake Company.** A final stop on this morning tour of Dockyard would be at the **Clocktower Mall** which offers dozens of affordable gift and souvenir shops, most of which are open 7 days a week.

From dockyard you can hop on a bus towards nearby Somerset, a quiet bay-side village with a definite British colonial vibe. The town itself offers little besides nice photo opportunities and few shops, but a lunch at either the **Somerset Country Squire** or the **Salt Rock Grill** would be a good simple dining suggestion.

Nearby and well within walking distance is the **Mangrove Marina** which not only is the departure zone for half day sailing and snorkelling adventures, but in high season the marina rents out Boston Whaler motor boats, wind-surfing, sunfish sail boats and sea kayaks at very reasonable rates. Check with your concierge to

see what special excursions are offered from this area on the day you are visiting.

From the wharf you can walk down the block to **Cambridge Beaches** *(photo on left)*, one of Bermuda's finest and most private resorts. Better call ahead and try to book an excellent spa treatment at its famed **Ocean Spa**.

Although another short bus ride (or 20 minute walk) away, additional sights in the area also include **Scaur Hill Fort Park**. Here you will find 22 acres of beautifully manicured hilltop grounds where visitors can tour Fort Scaur, a polygonal shaped fortress built by British Royal Engineers in the 19th century. Also nearby is the famous **Somerset Bridge**, the worlds smallest draw bridge.

You can either hop on a bus to return to your hotel, or if you want to enjoy a superb dinner nearby, hop on a bus and head over to the **Pompano Beach Club** (be sure to call ahead and ask for a ride from the main road) which offers two superb restaurants, both beautifully situated facing sea, just next to the stunning **Port Royal Golf Course**.

DAY 4
St. George & Vicinity
This tiny town on the eastern edge of Bermuda offers a unique sense of history and cozy charm. Originally settled in the early 17 century by a small group of shipwrecked English crewmen, this was Bermuda's first capital. Nowadays this is still a sleepy town, except for when the massive cruise ships dock here and unload swarms of tourists.

Start your visit to **St. George** at the harbour-front plaza known as **King's Square**. While the cruise ship passengers flock to the pubs and replica **Stocks & Pillory** here and along **Water Street**, there are plenty of other sights all within walking distance from the boutique lined town center.

An alternative route around the town and its surroundings would actually start out by the **Unfinished Church**. From here I would continue on a 15 minute uphill walk through the golf course and onto historic **Fort St. Catherine**. Besides the chance to tour a "haunted" old fort & its amusing little museum, just steps away is the superb shallow cove **Tobacco Bay Beach** complete with offshore cliffs just offshore. Your best bet around this part of

St. George for a decent lunch may beachside over at Tobacco Bay's rustic seaside snack shop.

After you've had enough fun in the sun, depart the beach and head back into the center of town. After you have seen all the shops and a few other historical sights such as the **Tucker House** museum and perhaps the **Bermuda Perfumery**, its time to hop on a bus or ferry back towards your hotel or cruise ship before it gets dark.

If you are staying at accommodations in St. George itself, try dinner over at either the laid-back **Tavern by the Sea**, or the more formal **Carriage House**. Also remember that on summertime Tuesday evenings from 7pm until 10pm the town of St. George hosts small but enjoyable **Harbour Night** street festivals.

DAY 5
Seaside Parks, Vast Gardens & Hilltop Mansions

The schedule for today starts out with a morning visit to the 36 acre **Bermuda Botanical Gardens** on South Road, which contains a vast array of flowers and exotic trees. Located in a pavilion within the Botanical Gardens is the brand new **Masterworks Museum Gallery of Bermuda Art** with its collection of superb paintings by internationally recognized local and visiting artists. One hour free walking tours of the Gardens depart at 10:30am each Tuesday and Friday

From here it's a short ride west along South Road to reach Collector's Hill Road where you take a brisk uphill walk up to visit **Verdmont**. Dating back to 1710, this beautiful hilltop mansion museum is filled antique period furnishings, Georgian era artwork, that contain fine examples of Bermudian cedar cabinetry, old English furniture, original Chippendale cabinets and antique children's toys.

By now you have probably worked up quite an appetite, so I suggest trying the nearby pub and restaurant called the **North Rock Brewing Company** situated on South Road. This cozy spot offers huge lunch portions of well prepared international specialties with affordable prices.

Another short ride further west, also just off of South Road, is the 59-acre **Spittal Pond Nature Reserve**. This is Bermudas largest nature preserve and is home to hundreds of lizards, crab, and bird species. The impressive cactus lined nature trails here take you past a **Checker Board** of giant rectangular geological formations. Also along the paths is **Spanish Rock**, a large boulder at the edge of the sea which was engraved by Spanish explorers back in 1543.

The perfect way to end a long day of walking in nature would be to head over to picturesque **John Smith's Bay**. The bay is home to a wide sandy beach that attracts fewer tourists than locals to its calm waters. The beach also has a few shallow areas that are great for snorkelling. There's a lifeguard and an inexpensive snack wagon during the summer and public restrooms. If you are looking for a nice uncrowded beach to be left alone on while touring this area, then this is the place!

Now its time to head back to your accommodations, and enjoy dinner at a nearby restaurant of your choice.

DAY 6
Flatts, Bell Diving & The Bermuda Aquarium & Zoo
Today's destination will be the area around a small former pirate haven known as the village of **Flatts**, located o the edge of the Harrington Sound. My first stop would be over at offices of **Bermuda Bell Diving**, Bermuda's most unusual and compelling

sea excursion. This is an amazing guided walk on the sea bottom during which clients wear large brass helmets and can actually reach out and touch the fish in coral reef areas. They have both morning and afternoon departures (high season only).

A few steps away, near the bridge that divides the town, is one of Bermuda's most visited attractions called the **Bermuda Aquarium, Natural History Museum, and Zoo**. The complex offers a wide range of exciting exhibits including the **Bermuda Aquarium** wing with its 26 tanks filled spiny lobsters, tilefish, groupers, moray eels, sergeant major fish, sea anemone, blue angle fish, parrotfish, squirrelfish, bream, jewelfish, and other exotic specimens. After passing by the outdoor harbour seal pools, you will be led inside the **Bermuda Natural History Museum**. Here you will find well presented photos, maps, and diagrammatic explanations about the islands' volcanic origins, indigenous plant and tree life, migratory birds, ocean currents, seacoast, and interior lands.

After leaving the museum, you will then pass by a series of outdoor cages and pens that comprise the **Bermuda Zoo**. You can watch many unusual as well as common creatures from all over the world including otters, two toed sloths, alligators, iguanas, tortoises, and a couple of bizarre animals such as Malayan water monitors and Madagascar ringtail lemurs. The complex also contains a summertime children's petting zoo, a wildlife rehabilitation center for sick and injured wildlife, public restrooms, and a nice little gift shop. Admission here is valid for all wings and exhibits throughout the complex.

After you have seen the Aquarium and Zoo, a nice simple lunch may hot the spot. I suggest enjoying good pasta or pizza over in Flatts village center over at **Rustico's**, a very good casual place.

From Flatts you can now take a long ride along the scenic **North Shore Road** and then turn onto Wilkinson Road where you will find **Crystal Caves** and the **Fantasy Caves**, which are adjacent to one another. These are the most impressive of the area's many caves and include an underground salt water ocean feed lake. The cave's top and bottom of the caves are covered by limestone stalagmites and stalactites forming unusual patterns. Guided tours are given by shouting staff members who lead you down a long slippery staircase and onto a series of floating bridges. Don't touch the formations, or else you will be in violation of the law! The caves are open from 9:30am until 4:30pm daily (except for low season when it may close on Mondays and for the whole month of January) and the required group tours depart about every 30 minutes throughout the day.

From the Caves it's a quick walk or ride over to one of Bermuda's most famous watering holes, **The Swizzle Inn** *(see photo below)*. The second floor terrace here is the perfect spot to dine on hearty burgers and seafood plates while gulping down their infamous Rum Swizzles by the pitcher.

DAY 7
Chill Out!
Today's schedule is up to you! If you need more sun and sea, try hitting the beach, or alternatively if you haven't had the time to shop for gifts, head back into Hamilton for the day. Perhaps even fit in a round of golf or a massage at one of the island spas.

Maybe the perfect way to end your stay in Bermuda would be with a superb farewell dinner at one of the islands top gourmet dining rooms such as **The Waterlot Inn, Fourways, Ascots,** or **Beau Rivage**.

8. BEST SLEEPS & EATS

There are 17 different recommended properties throughout Bermuda which I have reviewed for this book (listed in my order of preference in each section) and an equal number that I have chosen not to suggest for various reasons. While Bermuda is generally considered to be a medium- to high-priced luxury destination, there are several places to stay which represent unusually high value for the money, and I have pointed them out in this chapter.

These accommodations are grouped into four distinct descriptive categories: **Cottage Colonies**, **Resorts & Hotels**, **Inns**, and **Guesthouses**. Breaking up these best places to stay in this manner gives you a feel for what to expect from these establishments. I have also listed the **very best restaurants** throughout the island, from informal to top of the line!

WHERE TO STAY

The following is a breakdown of my terminology for these diverse places to stay while in Bermuda.

Cottage Colonies

These uniquely Bermudan deluxe resorts usually are comprised of several detached multiple occupancy lodges which are referred to as cottages. The cottages themselves may contain somewhere between 2 and 12 independent guest rooms or suites, each with their own private entrance, private bathroom, and in most cases a nice patio as well. It is most common for these cottages to surround a main clubhouse which usually houses a restaurant, bar, library, TV room, and the reception desk.

All cottage colony rooms and suites are fully air conditioned, and have private phones, daily maid service, and offer a wide range of on premises facilities. In some cases your room or suite may have a small refrigerator to store cold drinks and snacks. Most cottage colonies offer special dine around programs, access to private beaches, outdoor pools, an excursion desk or concierge, safe deposit boxes, and privileges to most major golf courses. Several cottage colonies prefer not to accept children under 5 unless accompanied by a full time nanny. These are fantastically enjoyable places to stay, and offer visitors a chance to experience Bermuda at its finest.

Hotels & Resorts

These properties are usually large hotels located either on the sea or near a golf course which offer a full range of facilities and services. Most resort hotels have one or more large wings, which can contain up to 300 rooms each. This type of accommodation is perfect for people who want to spend plenty of time on site, and take advantage of the many on premises facilities which can include golf, tennis, boat rides, pools, discos, show lounges, social desk, boutiques, business meeting rooms, and multiple restaurants.

All resort hotels are fully air conditioned and each room or suite generally contains a private bathroom, cable television, hair dryer, mini safe, and a host of other amenities. Children of all ages usually welcome at these hotels, and several offer great kids programs. Although not particularly Bermudan by nature, this type of property is what most North Americans are used to staying in while on vacation or business.

Inns

To me, an inn represents a private home or mansion that has been converted into a B&B type of establishment. These properties offer great Bermudan charm and uniquely personalized service. All inns are air conditioned, and have an assortment of cute guest rooms with private bathrooms in either a main building or an adjacent cottage. Facilities and room quality differ greatly from one in to the other, but almost all of them have a breakfast room, TV room, home style living room, and access to off site facilities. Some of the inns have rooms with kitchenettes, while others may offer their guests use of the main house's kitchen. Most inns will gladly accept children and can arrange babysitting. Inns are a great way to keep your budget reasonable, and still enjoy romantic accommodations and first rate service.

Guest Houses

I use this final category to describe converted manors and houses which offer minimal services, facilities, and basic inexpensive accommodations. Even though the government may consider all inns as guest houses, I don't.

Guest houses are usually run by nice Bermudians who enjoy hosting visitors in their own private homes. Some units have kitchenettes, air conditioners, views of the water, and a private bathroom. Some guest houses prefer not to accept small children. Considering the fact these are the least expensive and facility-laden accommodations available in Bermuda, if you carefully pick the right guest house you can have a great time and get a little local culture at the same time.

Hotel Price Listing Details

For all hotels, resorts, cottages colonies, guest-houses, and inns I have reviewed in this book, the prices categories listed in this book are based on the most recently available rack rate tariff sheets (the full retail price), and relate to each hotel's least expensive room with private bath, if occupied by two people, and do not include taxes and service charges. Special discounted rates are also often available upon request. This means that you may easily find lower package prices by calling each hotel directly, or by visiting a travel agent. Of course you should expect to pay additionally for suites, deluxe sea-view rooms, optional meal plans, spa therapies, excursions and tips.

Lodging Prices

$$	=	Under $150
$$$	=	$150 - $250
$$$$	=	$250 - $350
$$$$$	=	$350 and up

Price ratings are in US $ per double room per night, not including taxes, and are based on each hotel's least expensive room rates in low season.

In most cases the 7.25% government hotel occupancy tax, a 10-15% service charge (in lieu of tipping), and other nonsense surcharges (such as the so-called resort levy or energy surcharges, which are a complete ripoff) may be added to your bill.

You'll also see initials next to a reviewed hotel's rate that will help you to understand what is included in the lowest listed price in both high and low seasons. Keep in mind that while most hotels and inns consider April through October to be high season, and November through March to be low season, some properties do not necessarily follow this rule and may consider holiday time periods as high season as well.

Meal Plans Included in Price Ratings
• **E.P. (European Plan)** indicates that no meals are included.
• **C.P. (Continental Plan)** means that a small breakfast is included.
• **B.P. (Bermuda Plan)** suggests that a typical Bermudan breakfast will be served.
• **M.A.P. (Modified American Plan)** a full breakfast and a full dinner is included.

Some hotels also offer alternative or optional meal plans (including fine gourmet dine around programs) for a reasonable additional daily surcharge.

BEST COTTAGE COLONIES

POMPANO BEACH CLUB
Southampton $$$$ - M.A.P.

The Pompano Beach Club is Bermuda's best full service casual resort and is my favorite place to stay in all of Bermuda. This wonderful medium-sized property offers 74 ocean-view rooms within ten charming pink and white low-rise cottages, all on the edge of a bluff which rises up to expose dramatic views of the turquoise colored waters of the Atlantic.

Each cottage contains several spacious and comfortable double rooms and stunning suites (many of which can be made to adjoin for family usage) that feature individually controlled reverse cycle air conditioners, large deluxe private bathrooms, Mexican tiled balconies with patio furnishings and panoramic views out to sea, beautiful selection of hardwood and tropical rattan furnishings, king and twin sized Simmons bedding, hair dryers, direct dial telephones, 50 channel satellite-cable televisions, electronic mini-safe systems, mini-refrigerators, hair dryers, am-fm clock radios, steam irons with collapsible ironing boards, com-

fortable waffled cotton bathrobes, and large picture windows or sliding French doors that open up onto terraces with unforgettable views of the sea.

Tom and Larry Lamb are the friendly owners & managers and have done a wonderful job in converting their father's quaint little fishing lodge into one of the world's most relaxing and laid back beach-side resorts. The recent elongation of their tranquil private and unusually calm pink beach has made Pompano even more desirable for those who love the sand and sea.

The Pompano Beach Club offers a large heated outdoor freshwater swimming pool, several seaside sundecks with complimentary lounge chair and sun umbrella service, two open air seaview hot tubs, an oceanfront wading pool, four all weather and one har-tru tennis courts, a fully equipped health, guest membership privileges at all of Bermuda's world-class golf clubs including the adjacent Robert Trent Jones-designed Port Royal Golf Course, a fantastic water-sports center where you can rent all sorts of water-craft and snorkeling gear during the high season, on-site scooter and bicycle rental, free use of professional fishing tackle (the chefs here will be glad to cook up your very own catch of the day), express laundry and dry cleaning, available baby-sitters, breakfast in bed, and much, much more. If there is anything at all that you need to arrange excursions or day-trips, just feel free to ask for advice from any of the hotel's cheerful front desk staff.

Dining here is simply a fantastic experience. Even breakfast is a gastronomic delight, with huge cooked to order and/or buffet style American breakfasts served in the clubhouse, or a light healthy continental breakfast sent to your room. Hearty lunches on the sea-view Coral Reef Café terrace are one of the island's best values, while superb evening gourmet meals may be enjoyed at the lovely ocean-view Cedar Room and new Ocean Grill restaurants. Sunsets are also a delight with the added bonus a Monday evening manager's swizzle party, and sunset cocktail hours including scheduled live entertainment nightly by talented Bermudian musicians and local artists.

Guests may also take advantage of the Exchange Dining Program that allows them to enjoy gourmet dinners at The Reefs and Cambridge Beaches at no additional charge. Those here on romantic escapes will be delighted by the incredible sunsets that can be viewed from almost anywhere on the property, including your room. *Info*: www.pompano.bm. 36 Pompano Beach Road, Southampton. Tel. 441/234-0222, Fax 441/234-1694. Toll Free Reservations (Hotel's US Offices) at 800/343-4155.

CAMBRIDGE BEACHES RESORT & SPA
Sandy's, $$$$$ - M.A.P.

Cambridge Beaches is Bermuda's most refined, exclusive and secluded luxury vacation hideaway. This breathtaking 30 acre private luxury cottage colony resort & spa is ideally situated on a beautiful narrow peninsula surrounded by a string of five crescent shaped pink sand beaches. With its new multimillion dollar face lift, including the addition of a stunning new travertine sundeck pool terrace, the resort is even more impressive. Located just a few short kilometers away from the historic Royal Naval Dockyard, this peaceful resort consists of several traditionally styled pink Bermudian cottages, each with one or more superbly appointed oversized accommodations.

Each of the 94 rooms, suites, and self-standing villas feature powerful reverse cycle air conditioning systems, giant marble tiled private bathrooms (most also have a great Jacuzzi), tranquil sea or garden views, private terraces, a carefully selected collection of English country style hardwood furnishings, imported designer fabrics, large mini-safes, direct dial telephones with voice mail and data ports, remote control cable televisions, irons with ironing boards, adjacent peaceful gardens, and plenty of windows that let in an occasional refreshing sea breeze.

Cambridge Beaches easily lives up to its international reputation as offering its guests spacious accommodations, gourmet cuisine, Bermuda's only true world class health and beauty spa, and an outstanding level of 5 star service provided by a superb staff. Whether you decide to reserve a private self-standing villa, or instead choose a luxury suite, you will find yourself in a state of

total comfort and relaxation within seconds of your arrival. Keep in mind that Cambridge has a very private and secluded ambiance, and to keep things tranquil it currently does not allow kids below the age of 16 years old to stay here, with the exception of the holiday seasons such as Christmas and Easter.

The resort is home to a twin level Ocean Spa center, which is covered by a retractable sun roof. Facilities include six specialized treatment rooms where both ladies and gents can enjoy an outstanding array of European style health and beauty treatments, ranging from Swedish massages to various forms of natural hydra and aromatherapies. The spa also has fully equipped exercise and workout rooms, a 30 foot long heated indoor swimming pool, new sauna and Turkish steam bath areas, whirlpool jet baths, a natural juice bar that offers light snacks, and a full range of special "Spa-Holiday" programs.

Additional in-house facilities include a large outdoor saltwater swimming pool with multiple sun decks (one which is clothing-optional), a complete marina with water-sports equipment and boat rentals, customized deep sea or reef fishing and scuba diving excursions, complimentary use of three professionally surfaced tennis courts (one can be lit at night), temporary membership privileges at all major Bermudian golf courses, a putting green and a croquet lawn, on-sight scooter and bicycle rentals, a wonderful lending library with countless novels and historical texts, a fully equipped business center with regally appointed private meeting rooms, an extensive room service menu (with the island's best cooked to order breakfast in bed), complimentary afternoon tea served with finger sandwiches and sweets in the Clubhouse, nearby public bus and ferry stops, a daily schedule of exciting activities, a Monday evening manager's swizzle party, and stunning grounds embellished by magnificently landscaped semi-tropical gardens with charming foot paths that also run along the coast.

During the warmer months there is also live evening entertainment, sumptuous outdoor Barbecue buffets, and much more. Elegant evening meals are presented by candle light in the opulent Tamarisk dining room while more casual meals may be enjoyed at either Breezes patio or at the seaside al fresco Shutters snack-bar when weather permits. Cambridge Beaches also participates in the Exchange Dinging Program so that those on the meal plans may reserve dinner at The Reefs and Pompano Beach Club at no extra charge. *Info*: www.cambridgebeaches.com. 30 Kings Point Road, Sandy's. Tel. 441/234-0331, Fax 441/234-3352. Toll Free Reservations (Hotel Direct) at 800/468-7300.

FOURWAYS INN
Paget $$$ - B.P.

This peaceful little deluxe cottage colony rests on a private harbor-view estate in the heart of Paget Parish. Fourways Inn and Cottage Colony consists of several adjacent two-story pastel colored cottages, each with a deluxe double room and a lavish one bedroom suite that can be adjoined to create a two bed/two bath private cottages. Each accommodation here has a deluxe private bathroom with dual basins and gold trimmed fixtures, giant garden or harbor view balconies, remote control large screen cable color televisions, marble tile flooring, direct dial telephones, a collection of antique and reproduction hardwood furnishings including executive style desks, individually controlled air conditioning systems, overhead fans, original Bermudian artwork, both wet bars and mini-bars, small hideaway kitchenettes stocked with cooking utensils, mini-safes, plenty of closet space, an assortment of high quality English hair and skin care products, dual hair dryers, retractable make up mirrors, plush bathrobes and slippers, irons with boards, and in some cases even exposed beam chapel ceilings.

Fourways is an exceptionally quiet and secluded cottage colony with the services and facilities one would ordinarily expect to find in much larger four star hotels. Among the many facilities are a large heated outdoor freshwater swimming pool and sun deck, full access to the nearby Coco Reef hotel's beach club, temporary membership privileges to many of Bermuda's best golf and tennis clubs, a complimentary in-room continental breakfast featuring freshly baked gourmet pastries, a complete range of special valet and concierge services, express laundry and dry cleaning, available secretarial and baby sitting services, and of course direct access to the incredible Fourways gourmet restaurant and Peg Leg Bar and luncheon room.

A special dine around meal plan with a variety of superb Little Venice Group restaurants all over Bermuda is also available. *Info*: www.fourwaysinn.com. Middle Road, Paget. Tel. 441/236-6517, Fax 441/236-5528, Toll Free Reservations (Hotel Direct) at 800/962-7654.

PINK BEACH CLUB
Smith's $$$$$ - M.A.P.

This secluded seaside cottage colony is situated on 16.5 acres of landscaped gardens that slope down to two wide sandy private pink beaches off the famous Tucker's Town district. The Pink Beach Club tends to exude a very private and exclusive vibe, and the guests are not the most warm and friendly, but the property offers 81 sea-view rooms and suites (many of which can be adjoined) in a series of colonial styled low-

rise cottages. All rooms and suites here have individually controlled air conditioners, private bathrooms, hair dryers, hardwood furnishings, balconies, color cable television, direct dial
telephone, walk-in closets with mini-safes, am-fm clock radios,
irons, available mini-refrigerators, toasters, hair dryers, and pull-
out sofas.

Among the many facilities here are a restaurant and outdoor
seaside dining terrace, a freshwater swimming pool with sun
deck, two outdoor tennis courts, a fireside lounge, business
meeting and reception rooms, express laundry and dry cleaning,
available babysitting, a daily high season schedule of activities
and live entertainment, on-site spa services, temporary membership privileges at many golf clubs, complimentary room service,
and of course 2 superb beaches with a fine nearby snorkeling reef
that is full of friendly fish. *Info*: www.pinkbeach.com. South
Road, Smith's. Tel. 441/ 293-1666, Fax 441/293-8935. Toll Free
reservations at 800/355-6161.

BEST HOTELS & RESORTS

THE REEFS
Southampton $$$$$ - M.A.P.

If I were asked to close my eyes and imagine a perfectly deluxe
and romantic beach-front hotel, The Reefs is exactly what would
come to mind. This charming seaside resort and adjacent condo
complex is one of the finest small luxury hotels anywhere imaginable. Perched just above a sun-drenched bluff that rises up from
one of the Bermuda's most beautiful pink sand beaches, this gem
of a hideaway has always been one of the highlights of my many
trips to Bermuda. Voted as # 1 "World's Best Hotel Value" for
three consecutive years by the readers of Travel + Leisure magazine, The Reefs has also been on Condé Nast Traveler's list of the
"World's Best Places to Stay" since 1997.

The property contains 65 spacious and well appointed (yet
understated) hotel rooms, suites, cottages (and a series of frac-
tional ownership condos) that all offer individually controlled air

conditioners, private bathrooms complete with a selection of fine English perfumed soaps and shampoos, tropical rattan furnishings, ceiling fans, direct dial telephones with unlimited free local calls, wet bars with mini-refrigerators, Mexican tile flooring, mini-safes, plush sofas, original Bermudian paintings, large closets, remote control cable televisions (available upon request), hair dryers, irons with ironing boards, a tray of complementary beverages upon check-in, and in many cases there are even private furnished sea-view balconies with beautiful vistas out onto a superb beach area. The accommodations range from nice double rooms to massive one bedroom suites with Jacuzzis, or nearby independent villa style sea-side and garden-side cottages with one or two bedrooms.

Guests may choose to relax on one of the beach's complimentary sun lounges before utilizing a fully equipped fitness center with free weights and state of the art Cybex exercise gear, a freeform outdoor heated swimming pool with sun deck, two professionally surfaced outdoor tennis courts, shuffle board and croquet areas, and much more. There are also membership privileges and discounts on Bermuda's best golf courses, dozens of optional excursions, private guide services, scooter and bicycle rentals, both breakfast in bed and complete room service menus, weekly manager's cocktail parties, opulent lounges and fireside sitting rooms, a well-stocked lending library, walking paths through lush semi-tropical gardens, and a host of world class sports and water-sports programs available upon request.

Dining at The Reefs is an equally impressive experience starting at 8am each day with one of Bermuda's best breakfasts featuring both a fresh fruit and cheese buffet as well as many made to order items such as omelets or fruit filled pancakes. In the afternoons and evenings guests can visit either the Clubhouse dining room or the superb (and more casual) Coconuts sea-front terrace (open only in high season), which both offer some of the county's most innovative gourmet cuisine and vintage wines by the bottle and glass. You may also wish to indulge yourself at the beach-side snack bar, sip refreshing drinks at one of two delightful bars, or just socialize during each afternoon's complimentary tea service. You can take advantage of the complimentary Exchange Dining Program that allows them to enjoy gourmet dinners at Pompano Beach Club and Cambridge Beaches. *Info*: www.thereefs.com. 56 South Shore Road, Southampton. Tel. 441/238-0222, Fax 441/238-1214. Toll Free Reservations (Hotel Direct) at 800/742-2008 US & Canada.

ELBOW BEACH
Paget $$$$ - E.P.

The magnificent Elbow Beach hotel is an opulent and luxurious large seaside resort. This regal island getaway has been welcoming the rich and famous with unsurpassed style and grace ever since it was first opened its doors back in 1908. Now operated by the prestigious Mandarin Oriental group of Luxury Hotels from Asia, the property has just completed the final phase of an extensive $40 million renovation and enhancement project that has assured its unique position as one of the world's most memorable four star resorts. Located about three miles away from the city of Hamilton on Bermuda's famous south shore, this posh and truly luxurious deluxe hotel is surrounded by over 50 acres of beautifully landscaped gardens that face directly onto a superb mil- long stretch of pink sand beach. The centerpiece of the hotel is a pastel colored five story main hotel wing with a lavish marble tiled main lobby area as well as two restaurants, a tranquil bar, and several plush sitting rooms and terraces. There are 244 well-appointed rooms and suites. Scattered throughout the rest of the garden-lined estate are an outstanding array of world class sporting facilities, a private beach club, tranquil walking trails, an additional 20 cottages each with several super-deluxe accommodations, as well as a few super-deluxe independent one and two bedroom villas for those seeking additional privacy.

The majority of Elbow Beach's beautifully decorated rooms and suites have sliding glass doors that open up onto sea-view balconies or garden-side terraces, individually controlled air conditioners, marble embellished private bathrooms stocked with English milled soaps and shampoos, fine antique reproduction furnishings, Spanish tile or ornate carpeted flooring, European designer fabrics, mini-bars, direct dial telephones with data ports, executive style desks, electronic mini-safes, 44 channel remote control color large screen cable televisions, am-fm clock radios, comfortable king or double bedding, large closets with irons and boards, plush cotton bathrobes and slippers, hair dryers, additional pull out sofa beds, and much more. The private

villas also feature giant living rooms, wet bars, remote control audio/video systems, wood burning fireplaces, exposed wood beam ceilings, overhead fans, and their own delightful gardens complete with hammocks and deluxe patio furnishings.

Elbow Beach Hotel offers an Olympic sized heated outdoor swimming pool with a new open air hot tub, giant sun decks with complimentary beach chair and sun umbrella service, a health club, a health spa and beauty center, five professionally surfaced outdoor tennis courts (two are lit at night) with a great pro shop, a full compliment of daily guest activities, half day supervised children's activity programs during the high season, over half a dozen different fully equipped business meeting or convention rooms with private reception areas, a couple of wheelchair accessible rooms for the physically challenged, on-sight scooter and bicycle rental, several boutiques and newsstands, daily afternoon high tea service, a Thursday evening manager's cocktail reception, optional baby sitting by the hour, an excursion desk, a putting green, temporary membership privileges at most Bermudian golf courses, a nearby public bus stop and taxi rank, Bermuda's best 24 hour gourmet room service, and the only real concierge service on the entire island.

The resort's amazing pink sand beach is home to a private beach club where you can enjoy complimentary use of Riviera-styled private cabanas, just lay back and relax on a comfortable sun chair to work on your tan, enjoy refreshing snacks and beverages over at Mickeys' bistro and sand bar, or perhaps even kayak along the turquoise seashore. During the warmest months of the year several attendants will deliver freezing cold towels and cocktails to you.

Dining here is a delightful experience with four unique restaurants. The open kitchen of the resort's new Seahorse Grill creates an impressive evening menu of Bermudian based European/Asian/West Indian fusion cuisine, in an inspiring contemporary setting complete with post-modern architectural elements. The sophisticated yet relaxing Verandah Bar and terrace offers its own unique blend of delicate Mediterranean-inspired international cuisine served in a stunning old world setting with live piano music nightly. Over at the beach-front's Restaurant Lido guests and visitors can enjoy hearty classic Northern Italian dishes in the sea-view dining room and terrace. *Info*: www.mandarinoriental.com/bermuda. South Shore Road, Paget. Tel. 441/236-3535, Fax 441/236-5882. Toll Free Reservations (Mandarin Oriental) 800/223-7434.

FAIRMONT SOUTHAMPTON PRINCESS HOTEL
Southampton $$$$ - E.P.

The Southampton Princess is Bermuda's top large-scale golf, tennis, and beach resort hotel. The Southampton Princess began life in 1972 when famed billionaire industrialist Daniel K. Ludwig decided to spend a good part of his fortune building an opulent modern-Colonial styled deluxe resort on Bermuda's beautiful south shore. This excellent full service resort rises six floors above a superb championship golf course with views over a picturesque harbor and a spectacular beach-front. Winner of multiple AAA "Four Diamond" awards for excellence in providing extremely comfortable accommodations and outstanding culinary

delights, this 597-room luxury resort offers more services and facilities than any other hotel on the island.

Besides offering guests discounted rates and preferred tee-off times at their own wonderfully landscaped 18 hole par three golf course, the hotel also features 11 professionally surfaced tennis courts, both indoor and outdoor swimming pools with sun-decks, a fully equipped health club with sauna, optional spa and beauty therapies, and of course a beautiful stretch of pink sandy beach with its own private beach club and seaside food and beverage venues.

Other facilities and special services here include an on-site scuba and water-sports center, guest services and excursion desks, a team of patient golf and tennis pros, round-trip private ferry service to the Hamilton Princess, over a dozen designer boutiques and logo shops, free shuttle service to all points on the property, a superb high season supervised children's activity program, a giant state of the art multimedia amphitheater, several opulent meeting and convention rooms, and complete schedule of free daily guest activities for the whole family ranging.

All of the nearly 600 peach-colored rooms and suites here are surprisingly spacious and contain individually controlled air conditioning systems, custom built tropical rattan and hardwood furnishings, large panoramic balconies with patio furnishings, private bathrooms, remote control televisions with some 30 channels of international cable stations, king or double beds, walk in closets with mini-safes, irons with ironing boards, executive style desks with direct dial phones and computer modem plugs, and lots of natural sunlight. The structure's upper floors are reserved as a special Fairmont Gold section where for an additional $100 per night above regular rates you have additional access to complimentary breakfasts, concierge service, an honor bar with free afternoon tea with light snacks, and private check-in services.

Among the best of the seven dining establishments are the luxurious gourmet Newport Room and the more affordable but equally impressive Waterlot Inn. Those desiring more casual dining may choose between the Windows on the Sound, the Rib Room steak and seafood grill-room, the beach-front Whaler Inn, Wickets Brasserie, or the beach Cabana bar. The evenings here are also quite fun at the Neptune Room show lounge featuring live entertainment nightly. *Info*: www.fairmont.com/southampton. South Road, Southampton. Tel. 441/238-8000, Fax 441/238-8245. Toll free reservations (Fairmont) at 800/441-1414.

FAIRMONT HAMILTON PRINCESS HOTEL
Hamilton/Pembroke $$$ - E.P.

Every time I stay at the beautiful Hamilton Princess hotel it seems to be even more enjoyable than the last time. This delightful 4-star waterfront leisure re-sort and executive class hotel is the only truly full service large deluxe property in Hamilton. Situated on a beauti-fully landscaped stretch of prime real estate and surrounded by the sea, a pictur-esque inlet, and lush semi-tropical gardens, this has become the fa-vored home away from home for many inter-national businessmen and quality minded va-cationers.

Built back in 1884, the Hamilton Princess has recently been bought by the Fairmont Hotel group and has been steadily upgrading the rooms and the facilities. There are 413 beautifully decorated rooms and suites contain antique reproduction hardwood furnishings, fully stocked private bathrooms, comfortable king or double twin bedding, direct dial telephones with data ports and optional dial-up local Internet access, 26 channel remote control color television, huge closets, delightful earth-tone carpets and fabrics, huge picture windows with either garden or water views, electronically controlled irons with boards, fire detectors, coffee makers, and in many cases there are also sofa-beds, mini-bars, sitting rooms, and amazing private patios with outdoor furniture.

Corporate guests have access to a special recently renovated Princess Club floor with their own private check-in, concierge, and complimentary continental breakfast, daily international newspaper, afternoon tea with cakes, and evening wine and cheese hour. Guests who are willing to spend an extra $100 per night are entitled to upgrade to the much better rooms in the President Gold wing, which allow them to receive complimentary breakfasts, concierge service, an honor bar with free afternoon tea with light snacks, and private check-in services.

Guests have access to a full range of service and facilities including complimentary use of a well equipped health club complete with sauna, a pair of newly resurfaced salt and freshwater outdoor swimming pools with sun-decks, a putting green, an amazing Japanese garden with tranquil walking paths, several lounge areas, and of course their famous scheduled private ferry service to the full range of golf, tennis, dolphin encounter, and beach facilities (as well as restaurants) at their sister hotel in Southampton. Additionally there are several designer boutiques, a tobacconist & newsstand, a beauty salon, optional massage, a full service excursion desk, a full service business center, in-house scooter and bicycle rentals, express laundry and dry cleaning services, and much more. For business meetings and receptions there are several conference rooms and regal reception halls capable of hosting almost any special event conceivable.

The main wing of the hotel is home to two restaurants. Harleys serves up simple International fare, while snacks and dinners can be enjoyed over at the Heritage Court piano bar and restaurant. *Info*: www.fairmont.com/hamilton. Pitts Bay Road, Hamilton, Pembroke. Tel. 441/295-3000, Fax 441/295-1914. Toll free reservations (Fairmont) at 800/441-1414.

GROTTO BAY BEACH RESORT
Blue Hole Hill, Hamilton $$ - E.P.

Grotto Bay is a pleasant and surprisingly affordable bay-front resort hotel situated on 21 acres of peaceful grounds in the Bailey's Bay area. The resort is comprised of a series of 11 modern 2- and 3-story terraced water-view lodges which surround the main reception and facilities building, each containing between 15 and 30 nice simple rooms and suites which are well maintained. All of the property's 201 bright and airy pastel colored rooms are identically designed and contain television, radio, telephone, mini safes, small refrigerators, hair dryer, coffee maker, comfortable bleached pine furnishings, and private terraces. Many rooms can be made to adjoin for family use, and there are three huge two-bedroom suites.

Facilities here include complete dining facilities, beach pavilion, private beaches, outdoor fresh water pool, Jacuzzi, a water-sports center, scuba dive shop, four tennis courts, on-site moped/scooter rentals, exercise room, nearby golfing, a small calm private beach, heated outdoor pool with swim up bar and sundeck, hot tub, natural caves to both explore and swim in, 4 tennis courts, and nearby access to all sorts of sailboats, windsurfing, waterskiing, snorkeling, and scuba. A full day supervised children's program with off-site excursions and kids-only dinners may also available during the high season.

Meals can be taken at either the centrally located Hibiscus Room, or at the Palm Court. A complimentary afternoon tea is presented in the lounge, while cocktails are served at the Bayside Bar & Grill. Grotto is a great place to stay for people of all ages that want true friendly island hospitality and large modern accommodations without having to spend big bucks for the experience. *Info*: www.grottobay.com. Blue Hole Hill, Hamilton. Tel. 441/293-8333; Fax 441/293-2306; Toll Free (Direct) at Tel. 800/582-3190.

COCO REEF HOTEL
Paget $$$ – B.P.

Formerly known as Stonington, this is a reasonably nice seaside resort hotel with rates that are much lower than some of the competition. All 64 rooms have sea-views, air conditioning, marble bathrooms, imported hair and skin care products, ceiling fans, remote control cable television, private balconies, direct dial telephones, mini-safes, stunning lithographs by famous

local watercolor artists, hardwood furnishings, ironing sets, and mini-refrigerators. While not a luxury resort, this may be a good choice for those that are looking for comfortable accommodations within steps of some fine beaches!

The accommodations are housed in a series of modern two story pink buildings near the sea which are a short walk away to the hotel's main reception building. Facilities include a large heated pool with sundeck, a fine pink sand beach, tennis courts, a main lobby with an adjacent bar and fireside library, and the fantastic sea-view Café Coco featuring good lunches and dinners prepared under the watch of Executive Chef Pritchard. The hotel offers optional meal plans with dine around privileges, afternoon tea, and a Monday night manager's cocktail party. *Info*: www.cocoreefbermuda.com. South Road, Paget. Tel. 441/236-5416, Fax 441/236-0371.

WILLOWBANK
Sandys $$$ – M.A.P.

Willowbank is a non-denominational, non-profit Christian hotel, welcoming all visitors to Bermuda. Located only a minute away from the Somerset Bridge, this peaceful modest sea-side resort hotel is situated on six acres of gardens that look out over both the sea and some tranquil gardens. The cottage style rooms (some are sea-view) are nice and comfortable, but tend to be a bit on the

New Luxury Hotel Coming Soon!

Although not complete at press time, a new luxury hotel will open in late 2009 in the exclusive Tucker's Town area: the opulent **Tucker's Point Club Hotel & Spa**. I have poked around the construction site and seen the interior design plans, and I can tell you that this is destined to become a major destination for many Bermuda visitors. With the owners poaching top level staff members from every fine hotel in Bermuda and well beyond, and a management team from Preferred Hotels, this mid-sized seaside resort should be very special and equally expensive. Have a look at the new website at www.tuckerspointhotelandspa.com and if it is open by the time you plan your trip to Bermuda, and if money is no object, you may want to give this property serious consideration.

basic side. The guests here are almost all middle age to elderly clients who prefer the ambiance of a medium sized full service Christian guest center.

Although religion is a prominent part of the resort, it is not overly imposed except during grace before meals. Don't expect to find a bar or even televisions here! Facilities however do include a medium sized freshwater pool, two 2 private beaches, two tennis courts, a great pier for fish feeding, guest laundry room, and big old cedar beamed public spaces and reading areas in their main manor. A good value for those who are advised as to what one should expect here. *Info*: www.willowbank.bm. Somerset Road, Sandys, Tel. 441/234-1616, Fax 441/234-3373; Toll Free (Direct) at Tel. 800/ 752-8493.

BEST INNS

ROYAL PALMS HOTEL
Hamilton/Pembroke $$$ - C.P.

Situated on a peaceful estate just a short eight minute walk away from downtown Hamilton, this pair of adjacent turn of the century converted traditional Bermudian mansions feature several spacious English country style rooms, mini-suites and one bedroom deluxe suites. Each room is decorated with a wonderful selection of both antique and reproduction hardwood furnishings, oriental rugs, fresh flowers, spacious bathrooms with either marble or hand painted ceramic trim, comfortable bedding, remote control cable color television, individually controlled air conditioning, hardwood furnishings, direct dial telephones with voice mail and data ports, available mini-refrigerators, quaint French picture windows with stunning garden views, and complimentary coffee and tea stations. The suites have been especially designed for visiting international executives and in some cases also contain small modern kitchens with microwave ovens and mini-refrigerator, as well as computer fax modem adapters.

Guests here may choose to enjoy a delicious home-cooked continental breakfast, as well as superb gourmet dinners at the opulent Ascots restaurant. Additional facilities include an outdoor swimming pool with sun-deck, several tranquil reading rooms, an intimate cedar wood paneled bar area, and optional scooter and bicycle rentals. The inn's accommodations were so delightful that I wanted to cancel my next series of scheduled hotel inspections and just stay here to relax for a week or two. Royal Palms is a truly warm and friendly place, where guests are offered a high level of individualized hospitality. *Info*: www.royalpalms.bm. Rosemont Ave., Hamilton, Pembroke. Tel. 441/292-1854, Fax 441/292-1946. Toll Free Reservations (Hotel Direct) at 800/ 678-0783.

OXFORD HOUSE
Hamilton/Pembroke $$ – C.P.

Of all the affordable English style bed and breakfast inns in all of Bermuda, this is the one I would put on the top of my list. Located on a residential street just a few minutes walk away from downtown Hamilton, this is a charming little. Each of its 12 spacious and bright rooms are traditionally furnished, exceedingly well maintained, and feature quaint floral interiors, televisions, phones, coffee machines, air conditioning and a daily continental breakfast. With the ability to add a couple of cots inside most rooms, families will be pleased to know that children are warmly welcome here. The inn has attractive public rooms, a central spiral staircase, and terraced front lawns. The personable staff always seem to be smiling, and are quite happy to assist each guest. This is one of Bermuda's undiscovered little treasures. *Info*: www.oxfordhouse.bm. Woodbourne Ave., Hamilton, Pembroke.

Tel. 441/295-0503, Fax 441/295-0250, Toll Free Reservations (Hotel Direct) at 800/548-7758.

AUNT NEA'S INN
St. George's $$ – C.P.

This charming family-owned and operated small deluxe inn is a truly special place to stay while visiting Bermuda. Located in a beautifully converted 18th century mansion on a peaceful historic lane a couple of minutes walk from the center of St. George's town, Aunt Nea's is in a league by itself. Originally operated as a simple cozy guesthouse for shipwrecked sailors by the late Mrs. E. Trew Robinson, Aunt Nea's is now run by her son Delaey and his wife Andrea. Together they have worked incredibly hard to transform the once simple guesthouse into what has become one of the most beautiful and welcoming small bed & breakfast inns anywhere.

Aunt Nea's features 11 imaginatively decorated rooms and lavish suites which feature Andrea's amazing hand stenciled cabinetry, individually control air conditioning and/or ceiling fans, twin or romantic four poster and canopy bed in iron and rare woods, the nicest hand woven rattan furnishings I have ever seen, stunning granite tile-lined private bathrooms (which in some cases have glassed-in shower areas as well as scallop shell sinks and whirlpool baths), Spanish tile flooring, a beautiful collection of Bermudian watercolors and photography, minirefrigerators, hair dryers, am-fm clock radios. Some units also have original exposed beams extending through the ceiling and offer tranquil garden views.

 Besides several cozy sitting rooms, lending libraries, a hand made local gift shop, and a television lounge filled with plush sofas and plenty of local charm, Aunt Nea's has a wonderful garden-view terrace that is the perfect

place to glance out over their limestone Moongate and sip a warm afternoon tea. With its close proximately to fine golf, shopping possibilities, good local restaurants, fine sandy beaches, and historic sights, Aunt Nea's is the best place to stay anywhere near St. George's. *Info*: www.auntneas.com. Nea's Alley, St. George's, St. George's. Tel. 441/297-1630, Fax 441/297-1908.

BEST GUESTHOUSES

SALT KETTLE HOUSE
Paget $$ – B.P.

This delightfully casual (and affordable) little bed and breakfast on the edge of Hamilton Harbor is a real gem. The Salt Kettle House is comprised of a main house and several smaller Bermudian cottages located on water's edge just an eight minute bus, ferry, taxi, or scooter ride from downtown Hamilton.

Inside the inn's main house there are four beautifully furnished rooms each with air conditioning, private full bathrooms, comfortable beds, nice collections of antiques, large picture windows, and plenty of sun. There are also four extremely spacious one and two bedroom air conditioned cottage apartments complete with fully stocked kitchens, private bathrooms, and even wood burning fireplaces in some cases. Every unit is uniquely decorated with bright French style soft furnishings, adorable collectibles, and is stocked with good novels to read at night. There is also a TV room and lounge area in the main house.

Although there is no restaurant on the premises, all guests are served a fantastic complimentary full breakfast complete with homemade pancakes, muffins, fresh fruit, eggs, French toast, bacon, cereals, juices, coffee, tea, and marmalade. All cottage units also have their own kitchenettes, while guests in the main house rooms can use the ground level common kitchen throughout the day and evening.

Other special features of the Salt Kettle House include ferry service to downtown Hamilton and other points, nearby swimming and boating facilities, lots of harbor-front lounge chairs, and more charm than I could possibly describe. *Info*: www.bermuda4u.com. Salt Kettle Road, Paget. Tel. 441/236-0407, Fax 441/236-8639.

ROSEMONT
Hamilton/Pembroke $$ – E.P.

Rosemont is a nice and centrally located medium-sized apartment complex with nice studio and luxurious 1-bedroom apartments, some of which can comfortably accommodate up to four people each. Situated on a hill above Hamilton Harbour with great views, this tranquil complex is about a 5 minute walk away from the heart of town.

Each of the 46 tastefully decorated units have full modern kitchens, color television, telephones with free local calling, new comfortable furnishings, air conditioners. and some of the suites even come with Jacuzzis. Based around a modern 3 story wing, some of the rooms have pool-views, while others have dramatic patios with panoramic views over the harbor. Just next door are a handful of traditional Bermudian cabana style buildings that house nice but more basic garden view rooms.

Under the caring direction of Neil Stephens, this fine establishment provides wonderful self catering accommodations for a lot less than what I would expect to pay. Many guests are corporate clients who come here for extended stays because the ambiance is so laid-back. Coin operated laundry and vending machines are located on site. I certainly suggest this property to families and couples alike. *Info*: www.rosemont.bm. 41 Rosemont Ave., Hamilton, Pembroke. Tel. 441/292-1055, Fax 441/295-3913, Toll Free Reservations (Hotel Direct) at 800/367-0040.

EDGEHILL MANOR
Hamilton/Pembroke $$ – C.P.

This cozy bed and breakfast style guesthouse is set in an old mansion on a lush hillside a few minutes walk outside of Hamilton. Edgehill's 7 large and airy guestrooms offer lots of sun, tele-visions, and either private balconies or patios. The top floor of the guesthouse contains three fine rooms which have partial harbor views and cute outdoor sitting areas. This is a truly affordable property with a loyal clientele base of Americans and Canadians who return year after year. Some of the rooms can accommodate up to four guests, and children are welcome here. A continental (home-made) breakfast is included daily, and afternoon tea is available upon request. The atmosphere at Edgehill is casual, welcoming, and rather low key, especially at the outdoor pool and sundeck. This is a very good budget selection. *Info*: www.bermuda.com/edgehill. 36 Rosemont Ave., Hamilton, Pembroke. Tel. 441/295-7124, Fax 441/295-3850.

WHERE TO EAT
I have used a simple formula to calculate **the price range of a typical meal for two**. The pricing guide is based on the current 2009 cost for two people ordering a 4-course meal from each restaurant's normal lunch and/or dinner menu, not including either a well indicated 17% service charge, or a +/- 15% tip in lieu of any service charge. Gratuities, wine, drinks, and the most expensive al la carte menu selections have not been included in this formula. I have listed these restaurants in my order of preference based on quality alone.

Almost all restaurants in Bermuda accept major credit cards, travelers' checks, and of course cash. Some of the better restau-rants still require that clients follow a dress code of some sort in the evenings. The most common dress code requirements are....

Informal means that you can wear just about anything you like. Jeans, shorts, T-shirts, and sneakers are acceptable.

Casual usually indicates that shoes are preferred over sneakers; Bermuda shorts are preferred over regular shorts, no halter tops, no bathing suits, and no offensive T-shirts.

Smart Casual has become rather commonplace, and it usually advises men to wear cotton or linen shirts with collars and neck buttons, shoes, Bermuda shorts with knee high colored socks, or long pants (not jeans). For women it can be slacks, skirts, blouses, dresses, sun dresses, and fashionable sandals or shoes.

Formal has several different connotations. In most cases this refers to men wearing a button down shirt, sports jacket, tie, and dress shoes. For women it can include full length dresses, fashionable suits, blouses, and dress shoes. In rare cases, you may find that suits or business attire is expected, but I have rarely seen this be the case except for state dinners and official functions.

Restaurant Prices

$	=	Under $50
$$	=	$50 - $75
$$$	=	$75 - $125
$$$$	=	$125 - $175
$$$$$	=	$175 and up

Price ratings are in US$ and are based on the price of two people each ordering a 4-courses meal, not including taxes or tip, from a-la-carte menu offerings. Note that some major hotels also offer optional meal plans (including fine gourmet dine around programs) for a reasonable additional daily surcharge.

HARBOURFRONT
Hamilton Area $$$$

This relaxed yet opulent harbor-front restaurant and its adjacent ultra-hip Sushi bar are currently the hottest dining rooms in Bermuda. Favored by Bermuda's elite politicians and visiting celebrity types, this superb venue is situated on a posh waterside pavilion at BUEI. The menu features a huge variety of Italian influenced gourmet cuisine, as well as offering a separate world-class Sushi Bar with a slightly more casual setting. Those choosing to dine from the Italian menu can also order Sushi. During

my last visit Maitre' D Pierangelo Lanfranchi made a few suggestions from the menu which turned out to be perfect selections for
my taste. We feasted on beautifully prepared and presented
dishes such as a subtle salmon tartare with tuna carpaccio, Sushi
rolls with salmon, tuna and Wahoo, mussels simmered in herbed
garlic and white wine sauce, a simply amazing linguini with
lobster and fresh asparagus in a tomato cream wine sauce packed
with rich flavors, a charbroiled veal loin with shitake mushrooms
and perfectly roasted potatoes, and several fine desserts such as
a Dark & Stormy truffle and Tiramisu.

Open daily for lunch and dinner, reservations are absolutely
necessary, and the Dress code here is Smart Casual, although
most clients tend to arrive fully suited up. The Harbourfront is a
wonderfully refined choice with top quality service and equally
impressive array of cuisine and fine wines. *Info*: B.U.E.I., 40 Crow
Lane, Hamilton, Pembroke, Tel 441/295-4207.

ASCOTS RESTAURANT
Hamilton Area $$$

Located in a magnificent old Bermudian mansion just a few
minutes' walk or ride from downtown Hamilton, Ascots has
matured into one of the finest unpretentious gourmet restaurants
in all of Bermuda. What continues to make so remarkably de-
lightful is that it offers a unique
combination of superb gourmet
European/Bermudian cuisine,
flawless personalized service with
a smile, and romantic ambiance.
Set amidst beautiful gardens of
scented flowers and hand-carved
stone fountains, this amazing little
bastion of gastronomy offers seat-
ing in their two intimate fireside
dining rooms which are accented
with chandeliers, as well as on ad-
jacent al fresco dining verandahs
and a cozy gazebo. Tables are set
with fine china, imported crystal,
silver, candles and fresh flowers.

The charming antique brass and Bermudian cedar-wood bar is beautifully designed and offers an outstanding selection of vintage Ports, single malt Whiskies, Cognacs, Grappa and exotic liqueurs.

Extremely popular for lunch, dinner and Sunday brunch, the menu is a fine example of modern provincial Mediterranean cuisine. Dublin-born Chef Edmund Smith's specialty is incorporating local produce, imported meats, and fresh regional seafood into his own interpretation of both classic and nouveau European recipes. His sauces and garnishes are delicate yet just strong enough to perfectly enhance the flavor of the dishes they are dressing.

The menu changes several times each year, but during my latest two evenings I was seriously impressed with their chilled Bermuda banana soup with almonds and black rum, their own home-cured local Wahoo gravlax in a lemongrass infused balsamic vinaigrette, warmed creamy Bermuda goat cheese wrapped inside marinated grapevine leaves, salad of roasted duck with cashews finished in a creamy raspberry sauce, soy marinated black tiger shrimp presented on a bed of citrus drizzled Jicama accompanied with mango-tomato salsa, an unbelievably tasty pasta St. Tropez with grilled Mediterranean vegetables and sun-dried tomatoes, Thai marinated sesame encrusted fresh tuna steaks served on glass noodles, and a superb classic sirloin steak with roasted shallots.

Desserts here are created and include mouth-watering banana and dark chocolate crepes, tropical fruit sorbet, and several other unusual creations of the day. Winner of multiple Best of Bermuda awards as well as other highly respected international honors, Ascots continues to set new standard for gourmet dining in Bermuda. Open 12 noon until 2:30pm (every day except Saturday) and again from 6:30pm until 10:30pm daily. The dress code here is Smart Casual and reservations are strongly suggested. *Info*: Royal Palms Hotel, Rosemont Ave., Hamilton, Pembroke. Tel. 441/295-9644.

FOURWAYS INN
Paget $$$$$

This magnificent restaurant originally started life in 1727 as an opulent mansion for famous sherry baron John Harvey of England (founder of Harvey's Bristol Cream sherries). Back in those days Mr. Harvey enjoyed inviting his friends here for lavish dinner parties of legendary proportions. His private estate was later converted into an elegant inn and restaurant, and now this incomparable establishment continues to feature a magnificent main dining room embellished with exposed antique cedar wood beams and stone arches, there are also several stunning semi-private dining areas, and the picturesque Palm Court dining terrace. Ever since being awarded multiple AAA "4 Diamond" and Wine Spectator "Excellence" awards, it is commonplace to find American politicians, members of European royalty, international movie stars, and reclusive industrialists dining here among the islands' most demanding vacationers.

On my last visit here I enjoyed a fine meal. The team of master chefs create outstanding al la carte menus each night that may include Beluga or Sevruga caviar served on ice, lobster salad with artichoke and snow peas, smoked Scottish salmon with cucumber noodles, seared scallops and giant shrimp on ratatouille with pesto sauce, charcoal grilled rockfish with black olive and lobster paste, fresh broiled Bermuda lobster, the best Chateaubriand imaginable, rack of lamb, grilled filet mignon, and a many other seasonal favorites.

To accompany your delicious dinner the outstanding sommelier will present each guest with one of the largest, most comprehensive, and expensive wine lists in this hemisphere which includes over 7,500 bottles from the world's finest vineyards. After your meal I strongly suggest trying at least one of the superb pastry chef's soufflés or other mouth watering desserts. This rather traditional gourmet venue is perfect for those looking for the ultimate in classic French inspired delights. Open for dinner daily, dress code is Formal. *Info*: Middle Road, Paget. Tel. 441/236-6517.

THE WATERLOT INN
Southampton $$$$

The Waterlot Inn, owned and operated by the Southampton Princess Hotel, is a beautiful gourmet restaurant, serving fine continental and Bermudian cuisine within a 325 year-old converted warehouse and inn at water's edge. Each of the restaurant's intimate candlelit dining rooms is adorned with period furnishings, antique cedar trimmings, old paintings of seagoing vessels, silver and crystal service, and lots of charm. As one of the best upscale restaurants in Bermuda, the Waterlot creates superb a la carte menus with such mouth watering choices as salmon tartar,

mussels Catalon with saffron and garlic, excellent Bermuda fish chowder, fresh Caesar salads prepared at your table side, pan fried Bermuda fish on a bed of mushrooms and arugula, perfectly grilled rack of lamb, and an incredible assortment of rich desserts such as mascarpone cheesecake with cappuccino sauce. On most nights there is live piano music which perfectly accompanies the fine meals, aperitifs, and vintage wines that the Waterlot Inn has become renowned for. Open 6pm until 10pm daily, the dress code is smart casual and reservations are suggested. *Info*: Middle Road, Southampton. Tel. 441/238-0510.

LITTLE VENICE
Hamilton/ Pembroke $$$$

Located on downtown Hamilton's charming Bermudiana Road, this great little classic Italian restaurant has long been a favorite of both locals and visitors alike. The exposed brick and molded ceiling panel interior offers and intimate setting in which to enjoy delicious made-to-order traditional Italian cuisine in style.

The extensive menu here includes a wonderful roasted antipasto with artichokes and eggplant beside Parma ham, their famous calamari which is so light and crispy it is hard to believe, a superb St. Giusto salad with grilled chicken breast and portobello mushrooms atop fresh spinach leaves, an authentic minestrone soup, vegetarian cannelloni filled with ricotta and seasonal vegetables, pan-fried tender veal scaloppini, grilled fresh swordfish, and all sorts of daily made pastas and pizzas. The desserts here are also delicious (especially the tiramisu), and the wine list is extensive. Service here is polite and prompt, and the overall experience is rather enjoyable. Open 11:30am to 3pm on weekdays and 6:30pm until 10pm daily, and the dress code is smart casual. *Info*: 32 Bermudiana Road, Hamilton, Pembroke. Tel. 441/295-3503.

CEDAR ROOM
Southampton $$$

This superb seaside restaurant is a large part of the magic over at the Pompano Beach Club. The Cedar Room and the adjacent Ocean Grill have become one of the island's best relaxing dining venues and are both filled with the kind of welcoming, warm, and subtle ambiance that I rarely, if ever, see in Bermuda's more formal gourmet establishments. The excellent chefs here display a bold style of incorporating the freshest possible locally harvested produce and a selection of top quality imported ingredients into typical Bermudian dishes as well as both innovative New World and classic European recipes.

The Cedar Room's fabulous five course dinner menu, which changes each day of the week, may consist of such mouthwatering items as chilled pear and Bleu cheese soup, broccoli &

stilton cheese soup, char-grilled Thai chicken with ginger sauce served atop smoked vegetable ratatouille, smoked Scottish salmon wrapped around herb-walnut cream cheese, asparagus risotto, escargots in garlic butter, Ber- is muda codfish cakes, Bermudian lobster stuffed with shrimp and mushrooms, Jamaican styled jerk chicken, sesame encrusted rack of lamb, classic filet mignon, grilled Mahi Mahi, pan-fried rock-fish filet topped with a shrimp and chive crust, and many additional vegetarian treats. On Monday nights the menu changes to fantastic barbecue buffet.

Desserts here are also a serious matter, with a great selection of freshly made masterpieces such as peach mousse, Linzer tort, black rum pineapple cream tart, chocolate Grand Marnier mousse, brownie cheese cake, strawberry almond pillows, frozen peach passion fruit parfait, and an unforgettable banana royale. Open 7pm until 9pm nightly the dress code is smart casual and reservations are required. *Info*: Pompano Beach Club, 36 Pompano Beach Road, Southampton. Tel. 441/234-0222.

RESTAURANT LIDO
Paget $$$$

Stunningly located on the edge of Elbow Beach, this beautiful and charming restaurant is a true delight. The Restaurant Lido is a delightful and classy beachside grill house with excellent gastronomic delights and dramatic sea views. During the warmer months the Café puts up a terrace awning so that clients can dine al fresco style accompanied by the sounds of cresting waves. The main dining room itself sis urrounded by giant picture windows with views out over both the sea and the remarkably landscaped hibiscus gardens of the resort at Elbow Beach.

The 40 or so candle-lit tables with white linen are exceedingly comfortable, and every plate coming out of the kitchen is beautifully plated. Certainly one of the island's most romantic settings for a fine gourmet sunset dinner, the exceptional menu here features chilled fresh fruit salads, Parma ham served atop sweet melon, sliced broiled chicken with mango and avocado in a light

Two New, Posh Restaurants!

Two more new top quality restaurants are now open in Bermuda! Just as I was preparing this new edition one of these two places opened up and the other is about to open soon. Since I only had a quick chance to sample very limited pre-opening menus at each of these venues, I can't really properly review either of them at great length, but I can say they were both posh and had beautiful interiors.

Beau Rivage will offer classic French cuisine at its finest, while the new Tucker's Point Hotal & Spa offers two exclusive new beachfront and golfside terrace venues with superb cuisine (*photo below*). Give them a try and let me know what you think!

• **Beau Rivage**, 27 Harbour Road, Paget. Tel. 441/232-8686
• **Tucker's Point Hotel**, 60 Tucker's Point Rd, Smith's. Tel. 441/298-4000

creamy curry sauce, an outstanding lobster salad in orange sauce, whole wheat penne pasta tossed with sautéed shrimp and zucchini, skewers of grilled jumbo prawns with balsamic vinegar seasoned vegetables, mint marinated grilled lamb chops, and an amazing seafood casserole slow simmered in white wine and herbed tomatoes. The wine list has many, many bottles from Italy, France, and the New World and is an example of great value for the money.

Desserts change daily, but are always incredible, and the service here is superior. An evening here will be remembered for years to come. Lido is open 12noon until 3pm daily (April through October), and year round from 6:45pm until 10pm daily. Dress code is smart casual and reservations are strongly suggested. *Info*: Elbow Beach Bermuda, South Road, Paget. Tel. 441/236-9884.

TOM MOORE'S TAVERN
Hamilton $$$$$

A fantastic gourmet restaurant near the Crystal Caves is located inside of an opulent 17th century mansion loaded with historical links to the legendary Irish poet Tom Moore, who spent several days writing in this house and its gardens back in 1804. The restaurant features several intimate dining rooms on two floors, and a beautiful wooden upstairs bar. The restaurant is embellished with casement windows, cedar walls, a fine central fireplace, beautiful imported fabrics, and the finest European silver, china, and crystal settings.

The French and Italian inspired menu offers delicious oysters wrapped in spinach and poached in champagne, quenelles with crayfish sauce, an unbelievably light scallop mouse, escargots with garlic, Bermuda fish chowder, cream of corn soup with sorrel and smoked scallops, zesty scampi broiled in wine and garlic, a superb parchment baked filet of sole, fresh Bermuda lobster, veal tenderloin flamed with sherry and shallots, an amazing sirloin steak flamed with cognac and peppercorns, lamb chops sautéed with truffles and herbs, roast duckling with raspberry vinegar, a daily soufflé, crepes Suzette prepared at your tableside, and a selection of fruits, pastries, sherbets, and cheeses which are brought by on a silver Parisian dessert trolley. An extensive 26-page wine list includes hundreds of vintages from all over  the world. Open 6:30pm until 10pm daily. Dress code is smart casual and reservations are suggested. *Info*: Walsingham Lane, Hamilton. Tel. 441/293-8020.

BLU
Warwick $$$

Perched high above the Belmont Hills golf course in centrally located Warwick parish, Blu is a hip and modern bistro and steakhouse with a menu that offers up touches of Asian, Italian and southwestern American influence. The dramatic penthouse dining areas and patio feature breathtaking views out over of much of Bermuda and the vibe (and clientele) here is trendy and vibrant.

Among my favorite menu items here are the shrimp ceviche, fresh Blue Point oysters, fresh corn chowder, gnocchi with cherry tomatoes, garlic wine infused jumbo shrimp stuffed with crabmeat, the roasted double pork chops, baby back ribs, the massive 32 oz. bacon cheeseburger plate, an assortment of thin crust pizzas, and a good selection of desserts such as their molten chocolate pudding and key lime pie. Very busy around sunset for after work cocktails, Blu has a menu which is certain to provide something for everyone to enjoy. Open for lunch and dinner daily (and Sunday brunch) the dress code is smart casual and reservations for dinner hours are required. *Info*: Belmont Hills Golf Club, 97 Middle Road, Warwick. Tel. 441/232-2323.

COCONUTS
Southampton $$$$

This is, without the slightest doubt, the most romantic place along the south shore of Bermuda to enjoy an open air sunset dinner. This pleasant windswept cliff-side dining terrace faces out past the beach onto an unforgettable panoramic view of the ocean, and is booked solid almost every evening. The mid-priced lunch menu consists of unusual chilled and hot soups, fresh fruit plates, tasty tuna salads, grilled locally caught fish sandwiches, veggie pitas, BBQ beef sandwiches, huge sirloin burgers, fries, onion rings, and refreshing ice cream desserts and cakes.

At dinner, the food is a more eclectic blend of exotic dishes from around the globe including imported goat cheese with onions and tomatoes, fantastic cod fish cakes (the best in Bermuda!), Thai curried beef, calamari antipasto, daily soup selections, Caesar salads, grilled Bermuda Wahoo, rosemary marinated leg of lamb, an impressive pasta with fennel pesto and vegetables, seafood with ginger and coconut on black rice, thick veal sirloin steaks, and much, much more. The wine list here contains an excellent selection of 18 or so moderately priced international vintages. Make sure to save some room for desserts, including the devilish chocolate Pot de Creme custard. Open 12:30pm until 2:30pm and 7pm until 9pm daily. May be closed in low season. Dress code is casual in the daytime and smart casual at night. Reservations are required. *Info*: The Reefs, South Road, Southampton. Tel. 441/238-0222.

THE CARRIAGE HOUSE
St. George $$$

This is a romantic mid-sized restaurant is housed in a former 18th century carriage house in the Somer's Wharf complex of downtown St. George. The massive structure has been beautifully converted into a series of vaulted water-view dining areas replete with old brickwork and hanging plants. In the warmer months, they may open up their wharf-side outdoor dining terrace. The restaurant has become the best in St. George with the help of great lunch, brunch, afternoon tea, and dinner menus offering such specialties as huge sandwiches, burgers, an unlimited salad bar, Bermuda fish chowder, the Bermuda Triangle of filet mignon with shrimp and chicken, prime rib, fresh local fillet of fish, roast lamb in Porto wine glaze. a superb Seafood stew pescador, vegetarian pasta, Steak Diane, and dozens of other fine selections which are quite reasonably priced. Desserts are also a treat, with a whole trolley full of tempting choices to choose from. They even offer children's menus and early bird specials.

Service here is polite and prompt, with a totally stress free ambiance. They also offer a superb Sunday Champagne brunch. Open 12noon until 4:30pm and 6pm until 9:30pm daily, the dress code is casual and reservations are suggested. *Info*: Somer's Wharf, St. George, St. Georges. Tel. 441/297-1730.

PORTOFINO
Hamilton/Pembroke $$$

Portofino is without doubt one of downtown Hamilton's busiest restaurants. This small and often overcrowded Italian restaurant has a lively ambiance, and a staff which seem to always be in a rush to go nowhere fast. As with all good things, a little patience is the key to enjoying this bustling eating establishment. When the high season kicks in, it is not uncommon to find long lines of tourists and local residents waiting up to an hour to get inside. Most who people come here seem to take advantage of the moderately priced items on the menu, which include hearty minestrone soup, a good Caesar salad, fettuccini Alfredo, pasta primavera, veal parmigana, steak pizzaiola, lasagna, plump chicken cacciatore, excellent risotto, and over a dozen kinds of delicious thin crusted pizzas.

This is a great place to enjoy simple classic Italian dishes, especially later at night. They also have a take-out section where dozens of locals line up for superb pizzas and pastas to go! Open from 6pm until 11:45pm daily. Dress Code is Casual. Reservations are suggested. *Info*: 20 Bermudiana Road, Hamilton, Pembroke. Tel. 441/295-6090.

SILK
Hamilton/Pembroke $$$

Located on downtown Hamilton's famed Front Street, Silk is a fairly new Thai fusion restaurant with a varied menu of exotically spiced Asian cuisine. This restaurant has a rich Asian interior loaded with dark teaks and bamboo accents. The service here is prompt and professional, and the menu offers classic Thai dishes like chicken mango salads, vegetarian spring rolls, glass noodle soup, several different curries, Thai fish cakes, fresh pan-fried Bermuda Wahoo with Thai spices, and many more offerings. I really enjoyed my previous visits here, and the plates are beautifully presented. Dishes can be cooked to order from mild to extra spicy! Open 11:30am-2pm weekdays and every day from 6:30pm until 10pm. Dress code is smart casual and reservations are suggested. *Info*: 55 Front Street, Hamilton/Pembroke, Tel. 441/295-0449.

THE LEMON TREE
Hamilton/Pembroke $$

Situated near the Post Office at the intersection of Par-la-Ville Park and Queen Street in the midst of downtown Hamilton, this delightful little yellow cafe is a great affordable alternative to overpriced hotel breakfasts and lunches. The cafe is owned by Jean-Claude Garzia, a world famous French chef who has won several famed awards, and who also owns the brand new Beau Rivage.

The small menu here changes often but usually includes freshly made American style breakfast and lunch items such as scrambled eggs and bacon, pot pies, roasted chicken, filet of local fish, pure fruit juices, strong coffee, and of course a wide variety of sandwiches and pasta dishes for those on the go. The food is rather good and the prices start at only $9.50 for lunch. This is a nice little spot to meet local business people and have a hearty meal during the morning or afternoon while visiting Hamilton. They also have a busy Friday night happy hour party in their terraced rear patio facing the park. Open daily except Sunday for breakfast and lunch. No Dress Code. *Info*: Church Street at Par-laVille Park, Hamilton, Pembroke, Tel. 441/ 292-0235

CAFÉ CAIRO
Hamilton/Pembroke $$$

Perfectly located on a second floor walk-up along Hamilton's Front Street, Café Cairo is a wonderful addition to the city's already varied culinary and nightlife offerings. This cozy Moroccan/Egyptian/Lebanese restaurant is imaginatively decorated with Arabesque furnishings and rich vibrant silks and oversized pillows. Be sure to check out their superb outdoor dining terrace. Open for weekday lunches, and dinner or late night snacks with abundant cocktails (it actually transforms into a chic dance club after 10pm), the menu includes such favorites as falafel, hummus, babaganoush, lamb tagine, shish-kebabs, freshly caught fish of the day with cumin and other exotic flavors, baklava and other Arab specialties. Open from 11:30pm until 1:30pm and again from 5pm to 3am. Dress code is smart casual, reservations suggested for weekend nights. *Info*: 93 Front Street, Hamilton, Pembroke. Tel. 441/292-4737.

NORTH ROCK BREWING CO.
Smith's $$

Located about two kilometers from the Bermuda Botanical Gardens, this wonderful English pub-style microbrewery, bar, and international restaurant is a true delight. This is a friendly and unusually affordable little restaurant that serves up some of the biggest and best casual lunches in all Bermuda. To top it all off, they just happen to brew as many as eight different delicious varieties of tasty European-style beers in the exposed copper fermentation tanks located alongside the tables. The restaurant has an outdoor dining terrace as well as a brass and dark wood panel lined main dining room and bar area. The menu here is a real mixture of influences from around the globe, but house specialties include their dark beer and Bermuda onion soup, the giant Mediterranean pasta salad with feta and tuna, tempura of Cajun spice marinated shrimp, chicken teriyaki kebabs with Thai ginger sauce, huge burger plates with fresh and crispy French fries, pan-fried snapper topped with bananas and almonds, lots of daily specials, and pasta primavera in a chunky tomato sauce.

Perfect for either lunch or dinner, work up a big appetite before coming this way for one of the island's top values in relaxed dining. Open 11:30am until 1am daily. No dress code, reservations are not necessary. *Info*: 10 South Shore Road, Smith's. Tel. 441/235-6633.

PARADISO CAFE
Hamilton/Pembroke $

When you've just about finished your morning shopping excursions through downtown Hamilton and you want to rest your feet for a while, head to the Paradiso and treat yourself to a great freshly prepared breakfast or lunch. This cozy modern high-end deli, bakery, coffee house, and rendezvous point has huge picture windows facing directly onto Reid Street and makes some of the best cold sandwiches and pasta salads in town. The 18 tables here are almost always full (average wait time of ten minutes for a table to become available) with locals sipping strong cappuccino and snacking on delicate dishes.

Their menu features dozens of favorites such as tuna sandwiches on French bread, cold pasta salad with pesto and black olives, shrimp and spinach quiche, fresh blueberry tarts, and both hot and iced imported coffees made by European machines. The portions are reasonably large and rather tasty, and the prices are moderate. Open from 7am until 5pm Monday through Saturday. No dress code, reservations not accepted. *Info*: Washington Mall, Reid Street, Hamilton, Pembroke. Tel. 441/295-3263.

LA BAGUETTE
Hamilton/Pembroke $

Located in the central core of downtown Hamilton, this wonderful sandwich shop and adjacent cafe is the best place in Bermuda to enjoy a gourmet snack (either to stay in or to go). Among the offerings here: an amazing crab cake sandwich with ginger mayo sauce, a hot pastrami melt with Swiss cheese and sauerkraut on rye bread, filet of chicken breast with honey mustard on fresh baguette, tuna salad in a spinach wrap, and several other daily offerings of sandwiches, soups, and other delicious offerings. Eat in orders cost about 10% extra with typical sandwich prices starting from $6.75 with chips on the side. Owned and operated by a respected northern European chef that demands high quality from his staff, this is a great place for lunch.

A great afternoon snack alternative when time is short and you are very hungry! Open weekdays for lunch 11:30am until 4:30pm. No dress code, no reservations required. *Info*: 16 Burnaby Street, Hamilton, Pembroke, Tel. 441/ 296-1129.

SWIZZLE INN
Hamilton $$
THE SWIZZLE
Warwick $$

With their perfect roadside locations amidst the many attractions of both the South Shore and Bailey's Bay areas, these extremely popular bar and restaurants are both packed almost all the time. The simple wood interiors are studded with patrons' business cards plastered all over the walls.

Besides turning out hundreds of pitchers each day of Bermuda's most potent Rum

Swizzles (thus the phrase "Swizzle Inn, Swagger Out"), they serve great pub fare including crab bisque, red bean soup, Caesar salads, conch fritters, Shepard's pie, gigantic Swizzle burgers, fish sandwiches, English-style fish and chips, onion rings, nacho plates, lemon chicken, coconut shrimp, and the famous Johnnie's bread pudding with brandy sauce. You can sit either in one of the simple dining rooms indoors, but if the weather is good I suggest opting for a table on patio. You can even play darts while you wait for your table. Open for meals from 11am until 10:30pm daily, no dress code, no reservations. Closed Mondays from December to March. *Info*: Blue Hill Road, Hamilton. Tel. 441/293-9300; South Road, Warwick. Tel. 441/236-7459.

RUSTICO'S
Devonshire $$$

Situated near the bridge in the heart of Flatts village, this delightful little Italian eatery is about the best place in Flatts to have a home-cooked meal at a good price. The menu here is long and includes five different salads, over a dozen pasta dishes, and all sorts of pizzas and burgers. Great for kids and adults alike, I suggest trying the penne with lobster, the pizza primavera, the fish cake or steak sandwiches, and the chicken parmigana. Dinner here will cost somewhere around $65 for two plus wine. A nice affordable place with great service offered up with a smile. Reservations are usually not necessary. Open daily except Sunday for lunch and dinner. Dress code is casual. *Info*: 8 North Shore Road, Flatts Village, Devonshire, Tel. 441/295-5212.

DENNIS'S HIDEAWAY
St. David's Island/St George's $$

Although far from most major tourist destinations in Bermuda, this is the singularly most authentic sea-shack style restaurant in all of Bermuda. If you want to see the way real Bermudian families used to cook, this is just about the place to find out! Mr. Sea Egg Lamb prepares an assortment of unique St. David's style locally caught seafood specialties inside his humble converted living room in what seems to be a scene straight out of the old Louisiana Bayou. The food here is appealing in its down to earth simplicity and I guarantee that you'll leave this restaurant with a life-long memory of the experience. Dennis' hand written photocopied menu lists such wonderful offerings as mussel stew, conk stew, conk fritters, a wonderful shark hash, fish sandwiches, fried shrimp and scallops, shark steak, and lobster when it's in season. For the big eater, I suggest trying any of their dinners with "the works," which includes samplings of several house specialties. Bring your own wine or beer with you as they don't have a liquor license. Open 10am until 2:30pm and again from 6pm until 10:30pm on most days. Make sure to call first to verify their opening hours on the day in question. No dress code, but reservations are required. *Info*: Cashia City, St. David's Island, St. Georges. Tel. 441/297-0044.

THE PARAQUET RESTAURANT
Paget $

The Paraquet is a nice big city diner style restaurant with a lunch counter and two adjacent rooms with table service for about 50 people. This is the perfect place to pop in for a totally down to earth home-made meal and prompt friendly service. The clientele here ranges from local office and hotel workers in suits, to off duty taxi drivers and tourists in shorts and T-shirts searching for an inexpensive tasty meal. The menu features typical items such as omelets, jumbo burgers, club sandwiches, grilled cheese sandwiches, BLT's, roast beef with gravy, T- bone steaks, deep fried scallops, grilled pork chops, codfish cakes, BBQ chicken fillets, ice cream sundaes, and what may very well be the world's biggest lemon marangue pies. The restaurant also has a large magazine rack, and can make items to take out. This is one great local eating establishment that serves hearty sized portions. Open 9:30am until 1:30am daily. No dress code, reservations are not necessary. *Info*: South Road, Paget. Tel. 441/236-9742.

THE UPPER CRUST/FOUR STAR PIZZA
Various locations $

This is a chain of pizza restaurants that has taken steps to go more upscale than their beginnings as humble pizzerias. These are perfect places for a simple, affordable lunch or dinner. Besides pizzas they also offer fresh cut salads and other specials, and their superb Somerset location also has an extended high quality complete dinner menu featuring seafood and steaks as well as a beautiful separate dining room. The pizzas are offered with a variety of different toppings are available at an additional surcharge. A large pizza for two with a few toppings (for eat in, free local delivery, or take out) cost around $24.75 or so. Open 11am to 11pm daily. No dress code, reservations are not necessary. Free Delivery (yes, even to hotel rooms!) to most parts of Bermuda. *Info*: 10 Angle Street in Hamilton/Pembroke, Tel. 441/295-5555; 65 Somerset Road in Somerset/Sandys, Tel. 441/ 234-2626; 55 Middle Road, Paget, Tel. 441/232-0123; 6 North Shore Road in Flatts, Tel. 441/292-9111; Duke of York Street in St George, Tel. 297-3434.

ICE QUEEN
Paget $

Ice Queen is nothing more than an amusing little fast food takeout shop that happens to be open extremely late. While the menu may not impress you, where else can you get a burger at 4:30am? The fun really gets started after 3am when the bars and pubs in Hamilton close. All kinds of blasted swizzle laden locals and tourists alike will line up here and feed their bad cases of the munchies. This is a great place to people-watch late at night. The menu offers decent pizza, cheap burgers, fried fish filet sandwiches, huge orders of fries, cold soda, and ice cream. Just about the only late-night eating spot on this part of the island. *Info*: Rural Hill Plaza, Middle Road, Paget. Tel. 441/236-3136. Open 10am until 5am daily. No dress code, no reservations.

9. BEST ACTIVITIES

Bermuda has a great selection of **shops** and boutiques, mostly centered around the city of **Hamilton**, the town of **St. George**, and the **Royal Naval Dockyard**. The same is true for **nightlife**, with most of it in and around Hamilton. Chances are that your hotel will offer something to do at night as well, with the exception of the small inns and guesthouses.

As for sports and recreation, there's plenty: sailing, snorkeling, bell diving, cruises, swimming, windsurfing and other great **water-based activities**. On land, Bermuda has some of the best **golf** courses anywhere, and **tennis** is big here too. You can do Segway tours, bicycle around, and of course just hang out on **beautiful beaches** and soak up the sun!

BEST SHOPPING

What to Buy

The best bargains tend to be in top quality European designer clothing, jewellery and timepieces, china and crystal, figurines, perfumes, and locally made craft products. Don't expect to be finding any bargains on imported electronic gadgets such as laptops, I-Pods or digital cameras.

Most shops are open from 9am until 5pm Monday through Saturday, but as I have mentioned in each regional chapter, some larger shops may be open on Sundays (especially over at the small **Clocktower mall at the Dockyard**), and during special holidays and festivals such as Harbour Nights when many retailers may stay open until at least 8pm. There are no large Shopping Centers here in Bermuda. Credit cards and travelers cheques are widely accepted island-wide. **There is no retail sales tax in Bermuda**.

Products Made in Bermuda

If you're looking to take home something which has been created in Bermuda, you have several choices. The most famous products that come from here include Outerbridge's Original Sherry Peppers sauce (used to spice up such dishes as Bermuda fish chowder), Gosling's Black Seal rum, Somer's Bermuda Gold loquat liqueur, Bermuda Rum Cakes, Davison's Bermuda fish chowder, Bermuda Perfumery made scents for men women, and a vast amount of locally- produced art, crafts and much more.

Duty-Free Shopping

Duty-free shopping is also offered at the two Bermuda Duty Free stores situated at the **Bermuda International Airport**. A valid international boarding pass is required to enter these shops. Several Popular brands of sunglasses, leather goods, perfumes, liquor, wines, watches, cigarettes, and other locally made specialties are available at somewhat reasonable prices here.

For those looking for a more comprehensive selection of rare wines and spirits, most liquor shops offer a much wider range of specialty wines and spirits which can be sold at duty free prices if you purchase a minimum of bottles at least 24 hours before you depart Bermuda. After prepaying for the two bottles of duty-free liquor, inform the wine shop of your exact flight or cruise ship details and date/time of your departure from Bermuda, and they will held "In-Bond" at the warehouse and then delivered to you at the airport or ship terminal upon to your departure.

Many other items such as antiques, collectibles, and locally-made objects are sold duty free in shops throughout Bermuda.

The current allowable Duty Free limits for travelers to the USA and Canada is 200 cigarettes and 1 litre of liquor if you were here for over 48 hours. Please remember that Cuban cigars are not permitted into the US.

Where to Shop
Below is a selection of the best shops and boutiques I have found throughout Bermuda. Whenever possible I have included prices on their best buys, and exclusive lines, which are both subject to change. Most of these establishments accept Visa and Mastercard, some take American Express cards, and they will all gladly take travelers checks or cash (and perhaps offer you a better price).

ART & ANTIQUES
Heritage House. Situated in downtown Hamilton, this cozy antique shop offers fine local and imported treasures & works of art. *Info*: 26 Church Street, Hamilton/Pembroke, Tel. 441/ 295 2615.

Bermuda Craft Market. Located in the Cooperage Building, this market contains a collection of stalls which sell local hand made cedar wood miniatures, candles, shell art, quilts, dolls, stained glass, perfumes, Bermudian condiments and spices, and all sorts of other gift items. Artists can also occasionally be seen demonstrating their craft in front of visitors. *Info*: The Royal Naval Dockyard, Sandys, Tel. 441/234-3208.

Dockyard Clayworks. Situated in a huge airport hangar looking studio, Island Pottery fires up a vast assortment of hand-crafted

Bermudian pottery daily. Among the best buys here are the lighthouse style night-light holders ($30 and up), angelfish ashtrays, floral vases ($25 and up), mini moongates ($18 and up), and oval house plaques. *Info*: The Royal Naval Dockyard, Sandys, Tel. 441/234-5116.

Bridge House Art Gallery. A cute little craft shop, art gallery, and museum where you can buy prints, watercolours, and hand made gift items by many local artists. There is also an exhibit by the Bermuda National Trust with period furnishings and household goods. *Info*: 2 King Street, St. George/St. George's, Tel. 441/297-8211.

Carole Holding Studio. These shops and studios operated directly by local watercolor artist Carole Holding and contain a variety of her delightful original scenic watercolors, limited edition collectable prints, regular prints ($15 and up), large matted prints ($45 and up), and local crafts. *Info*: 81 Front Street, Hamilton/Pembroke, Tel. 441/296-3431 and also at King's Square, St. George/St. George's, Tel. 441/297-1833.

Picturesque Gallery. I came here to see some of the finest photography in Bermuda, and I was not disappointed. Matted cibachrome prints from local master photographer Roland Skinner are available from $149 and up. *Info*: 129 Front Street, Hamilton/Pembroke, Tel. 441/292-1452 and the Clocktower Mall at the Royal Naval Dockyard, Sandy's, Tel. 441/234-3342

Birdsey Studio. This is the best place to find original works and prints by Bermuda's most famous scenic watercolor artist, Alfred Birdsey, and other members of his talented family. *Info*: Stowe Hill Road, Paget, Tel. 441/236-6658.

Windjammer Gallery. The Windjammer galleries offer a huge selection of original Bermudian and imported watercolors, oil paintings, silk screens, limited edition prints, cards, photographs, and a sculpture garden. *Info*: 87 Reid St, Hamilton/Pembroke, Tel. 441/292-7861.

Art House Gallery. This cute shop and gallery offers an assortment of landscape watercolors, hand signed lithographs ($15 and up), unique cards, and screen block prints by Bermudian artist Joan Forbes. She can also be commissioned to create custom works for demanding clients. 80 South Shore Road, Paget, Tel. 441/236-6746.

BOOKSTORES
The Bermuda Book Store. This family owned shop offers 2 floors jam-packed with nature guides, travel books, best sellers, and locally published volumes. *Info*: Queen Street, Hamilton/Pembroke. Tel. 441/295-3698.

The Bookmart. Everything from magazines and children's books to best selling hardcovers and paperbacks at reasonable prices. *Info*: Phoenix Center, 3 Reid Street, Hamilton/ Pembroke, Tel. 441/295-2640.

Ships Inn Book Gallery. They stock thousands of books including historical titles, romance novels, current bestsellers, huge coffee table volumes, and more. *Info*: Clocktower Mall, The Royal Naval Dockyard, Sandys, Tel. 441/234-2807.

CHINA, CRYSTAL, GLASSWARE & PORCELAIN
William Bluck & Co. This massive shop has an incredible amount of fine imported crystal, glassware, porcelain, and china from such manufacturers as Royal Copenhagen, Minton, Lalique, Daum, Villeroy and Boch, Royal Crown Derby, Chase, Spode, Ginori, and others. Among the best deals here may be the Orrefors vases ($125 and up), the Kosta Boda wine glasses ($75 and up), and pairs of beautiful Waterford candle holders ($115 and up). They also sell fine English antiques and European silver. *Info*: 4 Front Street, Hamilton/Pembroke, Tel. 295-5367 and at Water Street, St. George/St. George's, Tel. 441/297-0476.

Gibbons Company. Bermuda's largest department store features a superb basement level glassware and ceramics dept. featuring crystal, glassware and china by Denby, Lenox, Bormioli Rocco, Laura Ashley, Mikasa, Wallace, Reed & Barton, Thompson, and Shannon Crystal, all offered at a substantial savings over U.S. prices. *Info*: 21 Reid Street, Hamilton/Pembroke, Tel. 441/295-0022.

Vera P. Card. This is the place to go for all sorts of gifts and collectibles including their famous collection of Hummel and Lladro figurines, German and Swiss ship's clocks and watches, Majorica pearls, and other jewellery. *Info*: 11 Front Street, Hamilton/ Pembroke, Tel. 441/295-1729 and at 7 Water Street in St. George/St. George's, Tel. 441/297-1718

CLOTHING

Archie Brown & Son. Here you will find 3 floors filled with imported ladies and gents casual and fashion clothing and accessories including Pringle Scottish sweaters, Bermuda shorts made from linen ($45 and up), Kery Hope skirts, ties, Nick Faldo golf shirts ($115 and up) cotton sweaters ($20 and up), docker slacks ($35 and up), knee socks, kilts, cardigans, mohair/wool leisure rugs, and kids stuff. *Info*: 51 Front Street, Hamilton/Pembroke, Tel. 441/295-2928.

English Sports Shop. The incredibly polite and helpful staff of this fine store help you to pick the finest quality English linen

jackets ($120 and up), Bermuda logo cotton golf polos ($35 and up), ladies Bermuda logo cotton sweaters ($35 and up), linen blend Bermuda shorts ($42 and up) straw hats, ties, cufflinks, scarves, knee socks ($11 and up) and Shetland sweaters ($50 and up). Upstairs you can find Harris tweed and custom-made suits by Alaxandre of England. *Info*: 49 Front Street, Hamilton/Pembroke,Tel. 441/ 295-2672. and other locations including St. George and Somerset Village.

Cecile. Women looking for the most exclusive European designer ready to wear dresses, gowns, unique sweaters, suits, swimwear, and accessories will sooner or later find themselves in this fashionable establishment. Among the fine labels available here are Louis Feraud, Geiger, Ciaosport, Mondi, Basler, and many more. *Info*: 15 Front Street, Hamilton/ Pembroke, Tel. 441/ 295-1311.

Marks & Spencer. This long established UK based retailer is renowned for the high quality and affordability of its products. This store sells ladies and menswear, lingerie, ladies shoes, toiletries, tailored dresses and suits, dress shirts, blazers, trousers, and beachwear. 17 Reid Street, Hamilton/Pembroke, Tel. 441/ 295-0031.

Aston & Gunn. Aston & Gunn occupies a corner storefront on Queen and Reid streets where men and women can find fine clothing and accessories such as Arnold Zimmer linen pants ($120 and up), Pierre Balman shirts ($45 and up), sweaters ($55 and up), ties, Bermuda shorts, dresses, jackets, suits, scarves, and other fine imported garments. *Info*: 2 Reid Street, Hamilton/ Pembroke, Tel. 441/295-4866.

Stefanel. As with all other Stefanel boutiques throughout the world, this shop has a small but exciting collection of European men's and women's fashions including Italian sport jackets ($140 and up), woolen skirts, intricate shirts ($45 and up), sweaters, knitwear, trousers, grunge style collections, and all types of accessories. Even the background music here is trendy. *Info*: 12 Reid Street, Hamilton/Pembroke, Tel. 441/297-1357.

DEPARTMENT STORES
Gibbons Company. Bermuda's largest department store features 3 floors of clothing, home decorations, kitchenware, furnishings and lots more. Major clothing brands sold here include DKNY, Izod Lacoste, CK, Liz Claiborne, Jones New York, Capelli, Bali, Calvin Klein, and Geoffrey Bean. They also offer glassware and porcelain by Denby, Bormioli Rocco, Laura Ashley, Mikasa, Reed & Barton, and Shannon Crystal. The shop also sells many fine perfume and cosmetics brands such as Chanel, Guerlain, and Dior. On the top floor there is a delightful and rather affordable luncheon terrace called the Birdcage Café. *Info*: 21 Reid Street, Hamilton/Pembroke, Tel. 441/295-0022

A.S. Cooper & Sons. The huge main branch of this fantastic department store offers four floors full of surprises. Here you will find porcelain, china, crystal, glassware, and figurines at up to 45% off North American retail prices from Royal Doulton, Wedgewood, Lladro, Waterford, Belleek, Swarovski, Orrefors, Kosta Boda, Waterford Crystal, and Aynsley, as well as unique pieces such as Limoges hand painted Easter eggs ($130 and up), and Bermudian cottage music boxes ($70 and up).

The store also has an abundant selection of men's and women's fashions from Ralph Lauren, Polo, Architect, and others, European perfumes, scenic prints, children's clothing, and a wonderful outdoor lunch and tea patio called Romancing the Scone. *Info*: 59 Front Street, Hamilton/Pembroke, Tel. 441/295-3961, and various other locations including St. George and The Royal Naval Dockyard.

JEWELERY & TIMEPIECES
Crisson Jewellers. Crisson has been Bermuda's leading jeweler since 1922. Visitors and residents alike have always found innovative design, the highest quality merchandise, and substantial savings here. In their several shops you will find Rolex, Ebel, Movado, Raymond Weil, Rado, Concord, Tag Heuer, Seiko and Citizen watches – all at savings up to thirty percent below what you would pay at home, as well as similar savings on an exquisite collection of fine jewellery from some of the most famous designers in the world.

Crisson's vast selection of over 75,000 different pieces is the largest collection of fine gold and gemstone jewellery in Bermuda, and each and every piece has a lifetime warranty and a certified appraisal upon request. Fine jewelry names available exclusively at Crisson include Carera Y Carera, Mikimoto, Kabana, Charles Garnier, Aaron Basha, and many more. They are especially proud of their selection of fine European pieces, many of which include exceptional quality diamonds that are hand picked by Andrew and Peter Crisson (expert graduate gemologists). *Info*: 55 Front Street and 71 Front Street, Hamilton/Pembroke, Tel. 441/295-2351, and various other locations including St. George, The Royal Naval Dockyard and several hotel lobbies.

Astwood Dickinson. At this well stocked jewellery store you can find watches from Patek Philippe, Tag Heuer, Omega, Baume & Mercier, Tiffany, Movado, Swiss Army, Tissot, and their own brand  of Bermuda flower watches. They also sell a variety of fine gold, silver, and precious stone jewellery, much of which is made at their design studios. Among the unique items here are several unique gemstone gold rings, and a selection of beautiful chains, bracelets, brooches, earrings, pens, necklaces, wedding bands, and accessories on all price levels. *Info*: 83 Front Street, Hamilton/Pembroke, Tel. 441/292-5805.

Swiss Timing. Even though this small shop is a bit off the main drag of Front Street, it offers a superb collection of lesser known, and thus inexpensive, brands of European and Japanese watches at fantastic prices. They also have a nice but limited selection of gold jewellery. *Info*: 95 Front Street, Hamilton/Pembroke, Tel. 441/295-1376.

LINENS
The Irish Linen Shop. What a fantastic little shop! The pleasant salespeople here can assist you in selecting fine linens and lace from all over Europe including Double Damask and Le Jacquard Francais, and many bargain priced items such as hand embroidered napkins from Madeira ($22 and up), Bermudian made floral pot holders ($5 and up), and some of the most beautiful Irish linen tea towels ($9 and up). The second floor offers a selection of French fabrics by the yard ($29 and up). *Info*: 31 Front Street, Hamilton/Pembroke, Tel. 441/295-4089.

Dockyard Linens. This shop has a small but affordable selection of imported linen tablecloths, local crafts, handbags, and gift items. *Info*: Clocktower Mall, The Royal Naval Dockyard, Sandys. Tel. 441/234-3871.

LIQUOR STORES

Gosling's. When you want a good bottle of wine to drink while on vacation, or need to purchase your duty free in-bond liquor, this store carries almost anything you might want. Certainly the largest wine merchants in Bermuda, they offer thousands of bottles of all sorts of wines & spirits for sale, including '87 Opus One, '85 Dom Perignon, '83 Chateaux Margaux, '87 Castello Banfi Brunello di Montalchino, and of course their own Black Seal dark rum and less expensive wines and liquors from around the world. They also offer great duty-free prices on fifths or liters including Many single malts, Goslings 151 rum, Jose Cuervo tequila, Vintage ports, Kahula, Frangelico, Chambord, and more. Their small retail annex shop in Somerset still sells their own unique Bermuda moonshine, which is actually a very special aged & unfiltered Bermuda Black Rum (unavailable anywhere else in Bermuda!) by the keg, or by the liter, but only if you bring an empty bottle and cap with you. *Info*: 33 Front Street, Hamilton/ Pembroke, Tel. 441/295-1123, and various other locations.

Burrows Lightbourn. This is another good place to buy beer, liquor, wines, and in-bond duty free packages. For immediate consumption I suggest Piper Heidsieck non vintage Champagne, '84 Chateux Ducru-Beaucaillou Bordeaux , Glenmorangie Single Malt Scotch, and their wonderful Graham 30 year Tawny Port. Duty free offerings include fifths and liters of Ameretto Di Saronno, Barcardi 151, Tanqueray gin, Stolichnaya vodka, Cardhu Malt whisky, and Frangelico. *Info*: Front Street, Hamilton/ Pembroke, Tel. 441/295-0176, and various other locations.

LEATHER GOODS & LUGGAGE

The Harbourmaster. If you have bought too many gifts to fit inside your luggage, or you intend to travel again soon, this is the perfect place to shop for luggage. This great shop has beautiful imported leather and nylon luggage, wallets, handbags, and briefcases. *Info*: Washington Mall, Reid Street, Hamilton/ Pembroke. Tel. 441/295-5333.

PERFUME & COLOGNE

Peniston Brown. Peniston Brown is perhaps the leading perfume store in Bermuda. Among the many European scents available here at discounted prices are Jean Patou, Guerlain, Lauren, Yves St. Laurent, and Calvin Klein. *Info*: 23 Front Street, Hamilton/ Pembroke, Tel. 441/295-3755, also at King's Square in St. George,/ St. George's, Tel. 441/297-1525.

Bermuda Perfumery. At the Perfumery you will first be guided on a free tour through the perfume making process, and then finish up sampling their LiLi-Bermuda made men's and women's fragrances such as Oleander, Frangipanni, Easter Lily, Passion Flower, Bermudiana, Cedarwood, Bravo, Bambu, and Navy Lime. *Info*: 5 Queen Street, St. George/St. George's, Tel. 441/293-0627.

The Perfume Shop. This nice small yet well stocked perfume shop offers many top shelf products. Lines here include Hermes, Jennifer Lopez, Boucheron, Yves Saint Laurent, Davidoff, Vera Wang, Guess, MAC, Van Cleef & Arpells, and many more. *Info*: Clocktower Mall, The Royal Naval Dockyard, Sandys. Tel. 441/234-3903.

T-SHIRTS & SOUVENIRS
Riihiluoma's Flying Colors. Here you will find 2 floors full of T-shirts and unusual gift items which start at under $10 each. Most of the time they offer a buy 3 get two free T-shirt sales. This is a great place to find something cheap yet interesting to bring to your friends and family back home. *Info*: 5 Queen Street, Hamilton/Pembroke. Tel. 441/295-0890.

Bananas. This is another great source for cotton T-shirts and a variety of gift items like umbrellas, towels, and sweatshirts. Here you can either buy 6 and get 6 for free, or if you're on a cruise ship, look for the lucky cabin number on display here and maybe win something. *Info*: 7 Front Street, Hamilton/ Pembroke, Tel. 441/295-1106, and various other locations.

Treasure Chest. If you need to find reasonably priced memento, this may be the place for you. Here you can buy typical tourist items like silver pendants, lapel pins, perfume, coral and pearl jewellery, post cards, prints, and cute gifts. 3 Queen Street, Hamilton/Pembroke, Tel. 441/295-2288.

Crackerbox. Here you can buy inexpensive souvenirs like nice polished shells of all sorts, pendants, post cards, sunglasses, calendars, hats, Bermudian condiments, cedar figurines, and other knick-knacks. *Info*: 15 Duke of York Street, St. George/ St. George's, Tel. 441/297-1205.

Hodge Podge. This is yet another little souvenir shop that sells straw bags, pendants, local condiments, cover ups, sunglasses, T-shirts, posters, postcards, chimes, cedar carvings, and film. *Info*: 3 Point Pleasant Road, Hamilton/Pembroke, Tel. 441/295-0674.

BEST NIGHTLIFE & ENTERTAINMENT

Most nightlife takes place in and around the capital city of **Hamilton**. While a strong pub scene has always been available, recently there are new wine bars, Friday after-work cocktail parties, and a thriving dance club scene. Additionally, several out of town nightlife venues can be found in Paget, Southampton, and of course both St. George and The Royal Naval Dockyard.

The minimum drinking age in Bermuda is 18 years old, so expect to be asked for picture ID. On most weekday nights the pubs and bars have no cover charge, although on some weekends (especially when live bands or DJs are playing), you may be asked o pay $5 to $10 a head to enter. Expect to pay a cover charge of up to $15 per person at the hottest clubs.

Just after the offices close at around 5pm, there are several pubs in and near downtown Hamilton that offer good happy hour specials. A great spot to start off Friday night in Hamilton is the outdoor BBQ and happy hour gatherings on Fridays from 5pm until 9pm during the high season is either at **The Lemon Tree** on Queen Street or perhaps over on the harborfront terraces of the **Fairmont Hamilton Princess** hotel.

From the the action moves onto the most sophisticated venues such as the **Opus Lounge**, Tel. 292-3900, and the **Little Venice Wine Bar** on Bermudiana Road, or perhaps the **Fresco's** wine bar on Chancery Lane, Tel. 295-5058. If you love jazz, a small local hang out called **Hubie's Jazz Club** on Angle Street (just off Court Street in a somewhat tough part of town, Tel. 293-9287) as well as the **Little Venice Jazz Lounge** on Bermudiana Road, Tel. 295-3503, both have great live jazz music (and occasional jam sessions) on Friday and Saturday nights from around 7pm until 10pm.

Those wanting to take on the city's many pubs should start off over at the **Robin Hood** on Richmond Road, Tel. 295-3314, the

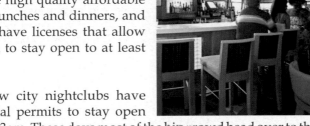

Hog Penny pub on Burnaby Street, Tel. 292-2534, or the **Pickled Onion,** Tel. 295-2263 (*photo at right*), or **Flanagan's**, Tel. 295-8299, both on Front Street. Most pubs in Bermuda serve high quality affordable full lunches and dinners, and also have licenses that allow them to stay open to at least 1am.

A few city nightclubs have special permits to stay open until 3am. These days most of the hip crowd head over to the **Café Cairo**, Tel. 441/292-4737, on Front Street to dance the night away, although **Level**, Tel. 292-1959, and Southampton's **The Cellar** both stay open quite late. Keep in mind that finding a taxi anywhere in Bermuda this late in the evening (even in Hamilton) is next to impossible, so either depart town before midnight, arrange a lift back to your hotel in advance, or expect a very long walk back to your room!

Other great spots around Bermuda to party and hang out include:

- **Swizzle Inn**, Blue Hill Road, Hamilton, Tel. 293-9300
- **The Swizzle**, South Road, Warwick, Tel. 236-7459
- **Frog & Onion Pub**, Royal Naval Dockyard, Sandys, Tel. 234-2900
- **White Horse Tavern**, King's Square, St. George, Tel. 297-1838

- **George and the Dragon**, 3 King's Square, St. George, Tel. 297-1717
- **Blu Lounge**, Belmont Hills, 97 Middle Road Warwick. Tel. 232-2323
- **Sea Breeze Terrace**, Elbow Beach, South Road, Paget, Tel. 236-3535
- **Black Horse Tavern**, St. David's Road, Hamilton, Tel. 297-1991
- **Veranda Lounge**, Elbow Beach, South Road, Paget, Tel. 236-3535
- **The Cellar**, Southampton Fairmont Hotel, Southampton, Tel. 238-8000
- **Henry VIII**, South Road, Southampton, Tel. 238-1977.
- **Somerset Country Squire**, Mangrove Bay, Sandys, Tel. 234-0105
- **North Rock Brewing Co..**, 10 South Shore Rd, Smith's. Tel. 235-6633

BEST SPORTS & RECREATION

BICYCLING
The typical price structure for a 21 speed Mono-Shock mountain bike is around $30 for 1 day, $50 for 2 days, $65 for 3 days, and about $10 for each additional day. Expect to also get hit with a non-refundable repair waiver of $10 and a refundable deposit of around $10. Some shops specialize in scooters and mopeds but still offer bicycle rentals with 2 or 3 days of required advance notice. If you ask, many will arrange a free shuttle pick-up from your hotel or cruise ship. The best places to rent bicycles include:

- **Bermuda Bike Tours** (Various Locations), Tel. 441/734-1653
- **Oleander Cycles** (Various Locations), Tel. 441/236-5235
- **Wheels Cycles** (Various Locations), Tel. 441/292-2245
- **Elbow Beach Cycles** in Paget, Tel. 441/236-9237
- **Eve's Cycle Livery** (Various Locations), Tel. 441/236-6247
- **Dowlings Cycles** in St. George, Tel. 441/297-1614
- **Smatts Cycle Livery** in Southampton, Tel. 441/295-1180

Or you can contact your hotel's front desk.

While there are miles of paved sea-view main roads throughout Bermuda, bicycles are also allowed on many sections of the Bermuda Railway Trail. For more details see www.BermudaRailway.net/.

BEST BEACHES

For many vacationers, it is the chance to bask in the sun on a beautiful pink sand beach that has brought them to Bermuda. There are actually dozens of impressive beaches to enjoy and explore here, especially between May and October when the turquoise sea can reach temperatures of up to 85 degrees Fahrenheit (29 degrees Celsius).

While many hotels and resorts have their own private beaches and swimming areas, many other fine beaches in Bermuda are accessible to the public and are often even more dramatic. Some of these beaches are perfect for socializing while you suntan, while others provide a more secluded and intimate setting. I strongly suggest visiting a few different locations, each with its own unique features.

Some of the more famous beaches (especially along the south shore) offer lifeguard posts, clean bathrooms, changing rooms, showers, snack shops, telephone booths, taxi stands, and snorkelling and beach gear rental shops. Public transportation can take you to most of Bermuda's fine beaches, and a helpful bus schedule and beach location map called *Bermuda's Guide to Beaches and Transportation* is available for free from the Visitors Service Bureaus. Remember that all beach houses, life guards, and facilities may be closed during the low season.

I've listed my favorite beaches on the next few pages. Let me know what you think!

Elbow Beach
South Road, Paget

This long stretch of south shore coastline is protected by a series of offshore reefs. The resulting calm waters and small waves are easy to manage, and the water is filled with schools of small friendly sub-tropical fish. This beach is always busy in the warmer months. Although private, you can walk a few yards down the shore to the adjacent public beach.

Horseshoe Bay Beach
South Shore Park, South Road, Southampton

Horseshoe Bay is perhaps Bermuda's most photographed and famous public beach. The crescent shaped long pink sand beachfront becomes the daytime stomping ground for hundreds of singles and couples during the summer. The water here is deep blue with medium sized waves and a brisk undercurrent.

During the high season there are lifeguards on duty, a beach house with public showers and changing rooms, restrooms, an inexpensive snack shop with a lovely outdoor patio, a telephone booth, a taxi stand, and snorkelling gear rental shop. Admission is always free, and the crowd is rather lively.

Jobson's Cove
South Shore Park, South Road, Warwick

Here you will find a quiet and beautiful small cove beach, sheltered from harsh currents and large waves. Each time I come here I see only a handful of couples swimming and sunbathing on the pristine sandy beach between a series of large shrub-covered cliffs. This is an excellent place to get away from the crowds; admission is free, but there are almost no facilities available here.

Warwick Long Bay Beach
South Road, Warwick

With over a half mile of pink sandy beachfront set against a backdrop of grassy hills, Warwick Long Bay Beach (*photo at left*) is the longest beach in all of Bermuda. The relatively calm waters are sheltered from strong undertows and big waves from the nearby offshore coral reef, a part of which can be seen majestically rising from the sea. Compared to some of the other major beaches in Bermuda, this one is usually half empty. Facilities here include public restrooms and lots of parking spaces. Admission is free, and the people here are rather down to earth.

Astwood Park Beach
Astwood Park, South Road, Warwick
Set below a wonderful seaside park, this cute little cove style beach offers its visitors a chance to swim and sunbathe in absolute peace and tranquility. The pretty beachfront has soothingly soft pink sand, and the water is fairly calm. You can snorkel a little here, but the beach is more noted as the perfect location to enjoy a wonderfully romantic picnic and catch a few rays. Admission is free; there are almost no facilities.

Tobacco Bay Beach
Coot Pond Road, St. George's
Although a bit out of the way, this cove beach is a fantastic place to enjoy nature's unspoiled beauty. The beachfront here is a bit small, and faces onto sheltered turquoise waters and dramatic

sea rock formations which are an easy swim away. A small adjacent beach house offers public restrooms, showers, watersports equipment rentals, changing rooms, and a basic snack shop. Admission is free, but to avoid overcrowded days, come here on summer weekends (when the cruise ships are not in port).

St. Catherine's Beach
Fort St. Catherine, Barry Road, St. George's
This often empty strip of beautiful sand and sea rests just below the massive defensive walls of Fort St. Catherine and was once part of the private grounds of the now closed Club Med resort. It's an excellent beach for a good suntan or quick swim, but don't go out too far here, the currents are strong! The old Club Med beach house is now locked up, so bathrooms and other facilities are not available, but admission is free.

Shelly Bay Beach
North Shore Road, Hamilton
Shelly Bay is one of the nicest large beaches on the north shore of Bermuda. It has a great shallow and sandy sea bottom which

allows people to walk out way into the sea without even getting your hair wet. Since the calm beach is lined by trees, finding shade is not a problem here. Located away from most hotels and resort areas, this beach has become more popular with Bermudians than with tourists. A full service beach house contains public bathrooms, a snack bar, snorkelling gear rental shop, changing rooms, and showers. Admission is free, and weekdays are the best time to visit here.

Church Bay Beach
South Road, Southampton
This is a peaceful secluded cove which has a tiny pink sand beach studded with boulders, calm waters, and a rocky ocean surface that attracts an amazing array of semi-tropical fish species. There are no facilities at this beach; bring your own rafts, snorkelling gear, cold beverages, and towels. Admission is free.

Somerset Long Bay Beach
Daniel's Head Road, Sandys
This is a long sandy beach with shallow waters that are perfect for the whole family. Surrounded by a tranquil park and nature preserve, Somerset Long Bay is favoured by locals and tourists alike. As long as you don't mind a constant wind, this is a great place to spend the day getting the perfect tan. Admission is free, but there are no real facilities here except for public restrooms.

BOAT RENTALS & CHARTERS
Renting a sail or motor boat is one of the best ways to enjoy a summer afternoon of exploration. There are several providers of boats in all sizes for all skill levels including sunfish, windsurfing boards, sea kayaks, Boston Whalers, and O'Day Daysailers, as well as more exotic skippered motor yachts and charter schooners. A refundable damage and theft deposit is required for each rental, and gasoline is not included in the price. Not all companies listed operate in the off-season months.

Typical 2009 self-skippered boat rentals rates:
• Single Kayaks cost about $20 per hour
• Double Kayaks cost about $25 per hour.
• Windsurfers cost about $25 per hour
• Sunfish cost about $20 per hour
• Jet Skis cost about $65 per hour
• 17' Day Sailers cost bout $30 per hour
• Boston Whalers cost about $45 per hour
• 23' pontoon boats (10 person capacity) cost about $75 per hour

Boat Rental companies I recommend are:
• **Somerset Bridge Watersports**, Somerset, Sandy's, Tel. 441/ 234-0914

- **Aquatic Bermuda Boats**, Hamilton, Pembroke, Tel. 441/236-2200
- **Dreamcatcher Boat Rentals** , Hamilton, Pembroke, Tel. 441/533-7236
- **Dockyard Boat Rentals**, Royal Naval Dockyard, Sandys. Tel. 441/234-0300.
- **Mangrove Marina Ltd.**, Cambridge Road, Sandys. Tel. 441/234-0914.
- **Pompano Beach Watersports**, Southampton. Tel. 441/234-0222.
- **Salt Kettle Boat Rentals**, Salt Kettle, Paget. Tel. 441/236-4863
- **Rance's Boatyard**, Crow Lane, Paget. Tel. 441/292-1843
- **Blue Hole Watersports**, Grotto Bay Hotel, Smith's, Tel. 441/293-2915

CHARTERED & SKIPPERED YACHTS
Rates range widely depending on the vessel and the itinerary, but expect the starting price for chartering a catamaran or perhaps 41' ketch to start at just $125 per hour, while a 93' Italian-built luxury motor yacht can cost upwards of $875 or more per hour.

Contact the following charter companies for more details:
- **Sail Bermuda**, Tel. 441/737-2993
- **Bermuda Charters**, Tel. 441/236-5071
- **Golden Rule Cruise Charters**, Tel. 441/238-1962
- **Ocean Star Yacht Charters**, Tel. 441/238-0116
- **Sand Dollar Cruises**, Tel. 441/236-1967
- **Bermuda Barefoot Cruises**, Tel. 441/236-3498
- **Salt Kettle Boat Rentals**, Tel. 441/236-4863
- **Chelonia Catamaran Charters**, Tel. 441/534-9771
- **Ladyboats Charters**, Tel. 441/236-0127

BOWLING

There are only two places to go bowling in all of Bermuda. Rates are about $7.50 per game, not including mandatory bowling shoe rentals.

- **Warwick Lanes**, Middle Road, Warwick, Tel. 441/236-5290
- **Southside Family Bowling**, 1565 Southside Rd, St. David's, Tel. 441/293-5906

CRICKET

This is a serious sport in Bermuda, and can be watched at several locations between April and August including the **St. George's Cricket Club**, Willington Slip Road, St. George's, Tel. 441/297-0374; the **Somerset Cricket Club** on Broome Street in Sandys, Tel. 441/234-0327; and the **National Sports Club** in Devonshire on Middle Road in Devonshire, Tel. 441/236-6994.

The big event in Bermuda's east end versus west end cricket circuit is when as many as 13,000 spectators jam the **Somers Day Cup Match Festival** in late July or early August.

FISHING

Although some of the world's finest reef, shore, and deep sea fishing takes place off Bermuda year round, the best months to fish are from May to November. Since Bermuda is surrounded by plenty of reef lined coast, shallow seafront, and two major off-shore fishing banks (known as the Argus and Challenger banks), over 600 varieties of fish species may be found including blue marlin, greater amberjack, tuna, pompano, shark, wahoo, bonefish, snapper, grouper, mackerel, barracuda, parrotfish, grunt, triggerfish, chub, porgy, blue marlin.

No special license is required to fish off of Bermuda, but there are several regulations that must be adhered to. No spear fishing is permitted within one mile of shore, spear guns and scuba tanks may not be used to go spear fishing. Shore fishing is prohibited at most large public beach areas. Spiny lobsters may only be caught from September through March, and by Bermudian residents only. Protected marine species include whales, turtles, dolphins, porpoises, coral, sea rods, sea fans, conchs, scallops, Atlantic pearl oysters, helmet shells, and others.

If you're interested in participating for prizes in the year-round Department of Tourism sponsored fishing competitions, contact **Tom Smith** at the Bermuda Game Fishing Association, Tel. 441/238-0112 or at partomar@ibl.bm. They follow the rules of the International Game Fishing Association.

For those of you interested in **shore fishing**, you should try your luck at Spring Benny's Bay, Somerset Long Bay, Shelly Bay, West Whale Bay, and around the Great Sound. Local suppliers will be glad to point out their tips and favourite locations. Expect to spend about $15 per day or $65 per week for rod and reel rentals (plus a $25 refundable deposit), and $7 for a pound of suggested bait (usually squid or fry).

You can rent fishing gear from:
- **Four Winds Fishing Tackle**, 2 Woodlands Road, Pembroke, Tel. 441/292-7466
- **Mangrove Marina Ltd.**, Cambridge Road, Sandys, Tel. 441/234-0914

If you are more interested in **reef and deep sea fishing**, its best to contact one of the many sport fishing and charter boat companies in Bermuda. Most of these licensed boats are fully stocked with tackle, bait, fish locating sonar, fighting chairs, and several comforts including kitchens and bathrooms. Although prices vary, expect to pay about $900 for a half day (4 hour) charter and about $1250 for a full day (8 hour) charter, for 4 - 6 passengers depending on the specifics of the boat. Make sure you ask the boat's

skipper who gets to keep the catch. On occasion they can arrange a charter share; that way you can join an already existing group for about 20% of the full charter price of the boat. Who knows, maybe you'll break the record of Bill Bundt, an American who landed a 1,190 pound blue marlin!

Suggested Deep Sea Fishing Charters ...
• **Overproof**, Somerset, Sandys, Tel. 441/335-9850
• **Mako Charters**, Spanish Point, Pembroke, Tel. 441/505-8286
• **Reel Addiction**, Somerset, Sandy's, Tel. 441/799-9927
• **In Excess Charters**, Hamilton, Pembroke, Tel. 441/335-6248
•**Atlantic Spray**, St. George, St. George's, Tel. 441/735-9444
•**Playmate Charters**, Pembroke, Tel. 441/292-7131

GOLF
Besides hosting a vast array of professional and amateur golf championships and tournaments, Bermuda offers its visitors a wide range of 9- and 18-hole golf courses. These courses range from beginners level all the way up to world class championship courses created by famous designers. Keep in mind that proper golf attire is requested in most of these locations (shirts must have collars and sleeves, shorts must be Bermuda style, no sneakers, no jeans). Tee-off time reservations must be made as far in advance as possible, and at the private clubs you may be limited to specific days of the week as a non-member. Reseeding may take place anywhere between September and November.

The most popular time to golf is **between January and April**, when the wind is strong and the temperature is comfortable. Most golf courses will rent clubs and carts, offer private lessons with their pros, sell golf balls at their pro shops, and offer refreshments and snacks. Caddies are not commonly available, except at the Mid Ocean Club.

Some of the private high profile courses can be difficult to get a reservation without knowing a member. Let your hotel's social desk or concierge handle these bookings on the day you arrive. If you're interested in joining a tournament, contact any office of the Bermuda Department of Tourism or the Bermuda Golf Association in Hamilton at Tel. 441/238-1367.

These are among the best golf courses in Bermuda:

Mid Ocean Club
This is Bermuda's top golf club, and as you will see from the rates, it maintains a high level of exclusivity. Designed by Charles Blair

 Macdonald, this 18 hole par 71 champion-ship course of 6547 yards is the site of several PGA tournaments throughout the year. This is a rather private club, and either your hotel's concierge (if they have the right connections) or a club member may be needed to get you a tee off time here. The non-member price here is $200 per person each round, or $70 per round when accompanied by a member, plus caddies fees, which are mandatory and run $25 per bag and up. Lessons cost $60 per session. *Info*: Tucker's Town, St. George's. Tel. 441/293-0330.

Tucker's Point Club

This Charles Banks-designed private 18 hole championship par 71 course has 6440 yards of windy oceanview and elevated inland greens. When they are not hosting a tournament, the course charges $150 per person per round, and $26 per cart. Lesson run about $90 per hour. *Info*: Paynter's Road, Hamilton. Tel. 441/293-2040.

Port Royal Golf Course

This newly rebuilt public 18 hole, par 71 course has 6561 yards of well manicured terrain. Designed by Robert Trent Jones, the course is known primarily for its windy location and elevated tees. The prices here are $132 per person per round including a cart. Lessons can be reserved for about $50 for 30 minutes. *Info*: Middle Road, Southampton. Tel. 441/234-0974.

Riddell's Bay Golf Club

This beautiful private 18 hole par 69 golf course facing the Great Sound has 5588 yards of challenging greens and fairways. First established in 1922, this is the islands' oldest golf course, and manages to keep its links in perfect condition year round. Since the club is so popular with members and visitors alike, you must book tee off times well in advance. Green fees are about $145 per person per round including a cart. Lessons run $70 per hour. Special sunset rates after 3:30pm. *Info*: Riddell's Bay Road, Warwick. Tel. 441/238-3225.

Fairmont Southampton Princess Golf Club

The Princess course is a wonderful place to enjoy a great game of golf, and feel completely welcome by the staff and locals. This par 54 executive 18 hole course has 2684 yards of impeccable greens and fairways. Well maintained and studded with steep hills, this  is perhaps the best location to regain your skills before attempting to play on the above (longer) courses. Each round will cost $84 per person including cart, or $60 after 3pm, and lessons are $40 for a half hour. *Info*: South Road, Southampton. Tel. 441/238-0446

St. George's Golf Course

This beautiful yet windy 18 hole par 62 Robert Trent Jones designed oceanview private course has 4043 yards of small, fast greens. The weekends here are too busy, so try the more relaxing Monday through Friday time slots. Green fees are $100, plus $48 for carts. Lessons here go for $50 per half hour. Special summertime sunset rates after 2pm. *Info*: Park Road, St. George's. Tel. 441/297-8353.

Belmont Hotel Golf & Country Club

Belmont is a nice and easy 18 hole par 70 private golf course of 5777 yards. Since guests of this hotel are offered complimentary green fees, you may find the links to be packed on many days throughout the year. Green fees are around $100 including cart rental. *Info*: Middle Road, Warwick. Tel. 441/236-1301.

Ocean View Golf Course

Ocean View is a 9 hole government owned par 35 course with 2956 yards of well manicured fairways and elevated tees. Now going through the final phases of a massive refurbishment, this is becoming a fine place to get in gear for the 18 hole courses. Rates are $65 per round and $18 for a cart. Special late afternoon sunset rates year-round. *Info*: North Shore Road, Devonshire. Tel. 441/295-9092.

HIKING

Although it is entirely possible to spend your vacation walking down all the country lanes in Bermuda, I have a better suggestion. **The Bermuda Railway Trail** is actually a walking path built upon the former track route of the now defunct Bermuda Railway, circa 1931.

The railroad once ran for 21 miles starting from the Somerset Bus Depot and crossing the whole country, until winding down all the way over on the outskirts of St. George's on the other side of the country. Although this limestone cliff and hibiscus-laden 1.75 mile-long first section of the trail allows mopeds and scooters as well as pedestrians, all of the other segments are motor vehicle-free zones. The part of the tracks that once ran through the city of Hamilton has since been replaced by modern roads, thus making the trail only 18 miles long these days.

A useful 24-page pamphlet (maps included) entitled *The Bermuda Railway Guide* is available free at any Visitor's Information Centre, and it is the best source for descriptions and directions to the various sights that can be seen from each of the seven sections of the trail. All sections of the trail are always open, but don't walk on its secluded footpaths after dark.

On Wednesday mornings at 10am the local historian, antiques specialist and expert guide **Tim Rogers** hosts a superb walking tour that costs $50 per person. The tour starts with a guided private visit to Waterville, a superb 18th century Bermuda mansion near Hamilton where you see impressive antiques and explore wander through the estate's lush grounds and rose garden. The he moves along to nearby Paget Marsh's boardwalk, a tranquil wetland full of unusual wildflowers and bird life. This tour is scheduled by advanced request only, so reservations are required. He can also arrange expert private guided walking tours throughout Bermuda upon request! *Info*: Tel. 441/236-6483.

HORSEBACK RIDING
A wonderful 75 minute trail ride on the dunes and paths near South Shore's famous beaches is available for $80 per person. These folks also offer private English style riding lessons for $40 per half hour.

- **Spicelands Riding Center**, Middle Road, Paget, Tel. 441/238-4241.

JET SKIING
These days the safety issues involved with this sport, as well as the local objection to noise pollution, has allowed only a few companies to continue offering this activity. Instead of just renting these high speed vehicles, they instead offer water tours or safaris in small pre-scheduled groups. Expect to spend about $140 for a one hour guided tour with two people riding on one double jet ski. Reservations are required and children under 16 are not allowed to drive these wave runners.

- **Sea Venture Water Sports**, Middle Road, Southampton, Tel. 441/238-6881
- **KS Water Sports**, King's Square, St. George, Tel. 441/ 297-4155
- **Windjammer Water Sports**, Royal Dockyard, Sandy's, Tel. 441/234-0250

• **Fantasea Bermuda**, Hamilton, Pembroke, Tel. 441/ 236-1300

PARASAILING
Weather permitting, 2 companies currently offer exciting flights on powerboat guided parasails from about March through November. Rates average about $75 per person for a 10 minute ride.

• **KS Water Sports**, King's Square, St. George, Tel. 441/297-4155
• **Fantasea Bermuda**, Hamilton, Pembroke, Tel. 441/236-1300

RUGBY
Bermuda's weekend rugby season is hosted at the **National Sports Club**, Middle Road in Devonshire, Tel. 441/236-6994. The season culminates in the fantastic Easter Rugby Classic, also held at the same venue, which includes several international teams.

SEA-BASED EXCURSIONS
This is my favorite way to spend a summer afternoon in Bermuda. Be careful if you book this through your hotel's front desk or concierge because they make large kickbacks to sell you on the larger and less impressive tours.

Many of these trips are designed as either relaxing sunset sailings, parties on motor yachts, rum swizzle sailing adventures, or various theme cruises. Snorkelling trips will usually include visits in a couple of different spots (either the sea gardens, reefs, or ship wrecks) and maybe a stop at a beautiful secluded beach or islet. Lessons and all equipment are included in the cost. Remember to bring a towel, waterproof suntan lotion, and a bathing suit with you. If you want to see shipwrecks and reefs laden with countless varieties of exotic fish, and you don't want to get wet, your best bet is a **glass bottom boat ride**. This is the shortest of the sea-based excursions, usually lasting only about two hours or so.

Finally, the most bizarre excursions in Bermuda may very well be the **undersea walk** where adventure-seeking individuals can put on a brass and glass mask (large enough to wear prescription glasses under) and walk along the sea bottom among the fish and coral.

Most of the companies below run during the high season only, and will reschedule excursions if the water visibility or sea conditions are not acceptable. These trips may not depart every day, and credit cards are accepted by only a handful of these companies. Special arrangements can possibly be made to pick you up at a variety of wharf-side locations other than the listed departure point(s). The companies I'd recommend include:

Haywood's Snorkelling Tours
These folks offer a daily 3-hour snorkelling tour aboard their 54' glass bottom boat from $50 per person. Departures from Hamilton only. *Info*: Hamilton, Pembroke, Tel. 441/ 236-9894.

Bermuda Bell Diving
A 3-hour adventure including a sea bottom walk with an old fashioned Bell Helmet. Departs from Flatt's Village and costs $65 per person. Morning & Afternoon trips. *Info*: Flatt's, Smiths, Tel. 441/292-4434.

Jessie James Cruises
A unique 3-hour glass bottom boat based reef snorkelling tour from $65 per person. Departs from Hamilton only. *Info*: Hamilton, Pembroke, Tel. 441/236-4804.

Fantasea Bermuda
Several half-day and sunset Catamaran based sail & snorkel tours from $60 per person. Departures include Hamilton, Royal Naval Dockyard and Southampton. *Info*: Hamilton, Pembroke, Tel. 441/ 236-1300.

Coral Sea Cruises
These folks offer a daily 90-minute glass bottom boat Eco Tours from $30 per person. Departures from St. George only. *Info*: King's Square, St. George, Tel. 441/ 335-2425.

Aquatic Bermuda
Captain Tony and his crew offer a superb 2.5 hour glass bottom boat snorkel tour from just $40 per person. Departures from Hamilton only. *Info*: Hamilton, Pembroke, Tel. 441/ 236-2200.

SHALLOW WATER SNORKELLING
The south shore of Bermuda has many fine beaches which are perfect for shallow water snorkelling. The best of these is Church Bay Beach, but there are fish near almost any beach you find. Resorts and hotels such as Elbow Beach, Southampton Princess, The Reefs, Pompano Beach Club, and others have their own snorkelling gear rental facilities. If you're going off a hotel's property to snorkel, you may want to consider daily or weekly rentals any of the scuba companies above. Expect a mask, snorkel, and fins to rent for about $15 per day or $60 per week, with a mandatory $25 refundable loss and damage deposit.

SCUBA DIVING
Bermuda's excellent diving season usually runs from March through November each year. For those of you who are inexperienced in this sport, you can take a resort course and learn the basics on land, practice in a pool, and then go out for a supervised ocean dive. For those of you with a current PADI certification (bring your card!), there are dozens of wrecks, reefs, and caves to enjoy. One tank, two tank, cave, and night dives can be enjoyed with the assistance of several Bermuda based outfitters. On average 2009 price for a 1 tank dive including gear is $85, a 2-tank dive is about $120 and a 4-tank dive is about $200.

If you want to get certified in Bermuda, the cost is about $575 and the process takes about 4 days. Consider the purchase of a PADI diver accident insurance policy, and take all of the proper precautions, as there is only one decompression chamber at King Edward VII Hospital. A well-written pamphlet entitled *Bermuda – Where to Dive* can be obtained for free from any Bermuda Department of Tourism office. Try these dive centers:

- **Blue Water Divers**, Robinson's Marina, Sandys, Tel. 441/234-1034
- **Fantasea Bermuda**, Hamilton, Pembroke, Tel. 441/236-1300

- **Dive Bermuda**, Fairmont Princess Hotel, Southampton, Tel. 441/238-2332
- **Triangle Diving**, Blue Hole Hill, Smith's, Tel. 441/293-7319.

SPAS & RELAXATION

A select few hotels in Bermuda now offer a variety of spa services and complete health and beauty programs. These range from beauty treatments and Swedish massages to more complex and effective rake, aromatheraphy, and deep tissue sports massages. Expect to spend about $110 for a 50-minute massage or around $45 for a French manicure. Reservations are essential for any spa here, and I suggest if service is good that you consider leaving a tip of around 15% which will be shared by all your therapists.

A handful of the better luxury hotels, such as Elbow Beach, the Fairmont Southampton Princess, The Reefs and Cambridge Beaches have superb spas which can arrange massages for their guests for a cost of around $140 per hour. See Chapter 8 for contact information for each of these hotel spas.

The magnificent **Cambridge Beaches** resort in Sandy's Parish offers one of the most relaxing and inviting spas on earth. Complete with a lavish saltwater indoor swimming pool as well as a spa bar serving healthy snacks and fresh juices, this oasis of tranquility and relaxation has been selected as among the five best spa resorts in the world by the *Conde Naste Traveler* magazine reader survey. Besides incredibly relaxing Swedish and Hydro massages available for 25 minutes or more, there is a vast array of additional treatments available by the half hour, half day and full day such as Reiki, holistic Reflexology, plant extract Aromatherapy, facial therapies, manicure/pedicure masks, mud baths, hair styling, and other body beauty beautification therapies for both men and women.

I enjoyed several services here and by the time my 120-minute session was finished I was so relaxed that I just wanted to sit next to the sea and stare into the waves for a few hours, something I have never been calm enough to even consider before in my life.

DOLPHIN ENCOUNTERS

Dolphin Quest. is located within the walls of the **Maritime Museum** at the Royal Naval Dockyard on Bermuda's western tip. After their success with similar adventures in both Hawaii and Polynesia, Dolphin Quest is offering visitors the chance to experience a 30 minute (or longer) interactive dolphin encounter during which they can stand, float or swim inside the confines of a specially redesigned salt water enclosure and touch or swim with a series of trained Atlantic bottlenose dolphins.

There are several programs to choose from and they vary in length and price depending on your swimming ability, age, and budget. Prior to the actual encounter with the dolphins, participants learn basic information about these friendly creatures and their natural habitat. The experience is available to adults as well as children (at differing times), and is scheduled several times each day of the week all year long (wet suits are both available and required during the off season due to cold sea temperatures!) rain or shine. Also available at extra cost are behind the scenes tours, special interactivity programs, and more.

Due to the often heavy demand for space for these programs during high season, reservations should be made as far in advance as possible. There are also free lectures and kids entertainment programs scheduled at least twice a week. The Dolphin Quest interactive programs currently cost between $95 and $295 per person and opening hours are between 9:30am and 5pm every day of the week. Visitor's who have paid the entrance fee to the Maritime Museum may watch the dolphins at play for free during scheduled program times. *Info*: Tel. 441/234-4464, www.dolphinquest.org.

SOCCER

Soccer games are a common sight at school fields and public parks throughout Bermuda. Each April several North American and Caribbean national youth soccer teams compete in the Diadora Youth Soccer Cup on assorted fields in Bermuda.

SQUASH
The major squash facility is at the Bermuda Squash Racquets Club, Middle Road, Devonshire, Tel. 441/292-6881. Here you can play on one of 4 courts for about $9 per hour plus a $7.50 guest fee. Rental racquets and squash balls are also available.

TENNIS
Since its introduction to Bermuda in the late 19th century, tennis has become a vastly popular sport here. With well over 100 courts available at many large hotels, as well as an assortment of public and private clubs, you will almost never have a problem finding court time if you book it in advance. Many facilities (including listed resort courts) are open to the public and also offer rental racquets, ball machines, lessons, and may require tennis whites to be worn. These are among the best places to play tennis here:

* **Government Tennis Stadium**, Marsh Folly Rd, Pembroke. Tel. 441/292-0105
* **Fairmont Princess Hotel**, South Road, Southampton. Tel. 441/238-1005
* **Elbow Beach Hotel**, South Road, Paget. Tel. 441/236-3535
* **Tucker's Town Club**, Tucker's Town, Hamilton. Tel. 441/293-2040
* **Port Royal Golf Club**, Middle Road, Southampton. Tel. 441/234-0974

WATER SKIING
On warm summer days you can't help but notice several private boats pulling skiers along through the bays, sounds, and harbors of Bermuda. Visitors can join in the fun from March through November, and even take a few lessons. Expect to pay around $75 per half hour (including lessons) for groups of up to 4 people with all the necessary equipment included.

Try these places to waterski:

* **Robinson's Marina**, Somerset Bridge, Sandys. Tel. 441/234-3354
* **Island Water Skiing**, Grotto Bay Hotel, Hamilton. Tel. 441/293-2915

- **Fantasea Diving**, Harbour Road, Warwick. Tel. 441/293-2543
- **SouthSideWatersports**, Tucker's Town, Hamilton. Tel. 441/236-6339

YACHT RACES
During the year, Bermuda hosts an assortment of international and local races and **cup matches** between March and November. Check the *Festivals & Special Events* section in the next chapter.

10. PRACTICAL MATTERS

ARRIVALS & DEPARTURES

Airport Arrivals
A **valid passport is now required** for entry into Bermuda.

The vast majority of visitors to Bermuda will arrive by airline at the **Bermuda L.F. Wade International Airport**. Located on the St. David's Island on the eastern part of Bermuda, this modern facility offers free luggage carts, Bank machines, cafes, restaurants, telephones and a taxi/airport transfer stand.

Cruises
During the high season only (roughly May through October) there are up to five different luxury liners docked at the Bermudian ports of Hamilton, St. George's, and Dockyard. The vast majority of these cruise ships depart the major cities on America's eastern seaboard (such as New York and Boston) for five-to-seven day adventures that dock mainly at the newly enlarged cruise ship terminals at the Royal Naval Dockyard. They include an average of four days in Bermuda and one and a half days at sea in each direction to get to and from their points of departure.

While state rooms, pricing policies, and clientele vary between cruise lines, they all offer some of the same basic features. Once at sea on these floating resorts, you can enjoy formal dinners and massive midnight buffets, exciting casino action, live music and entertainment, fully supervised children's activity programs, plenty of duty-free shopping, on-board movie theaters, sea-view lounges, optional baby sitting services, free 24 hour room service, sporting events, theme parties, sun bathing, socializing, and plenty of other fun-filled scheduled activities each day. Their rates include as many as eight meals per day ranging from formal gala dinners to massive casual midnight buffets (even when you are docked at port), and for a small surcharge a number of optional day trips and excursions in Bermuda may be arranged.

Keep in mind that port charges, government departure taxes and fuel surcharges may add up to over $205 per person (including children) which may be included in most cruises' advertised prices, so ask for details before you reserve your space. Tippingcould come to more than $75 per passenger per cruise. The three major cruise lines operating to Bermuda are:

- **Norwegian Cruise Lines**, www.ncl.com. Tel. 866/234-7350
- **Royal Caribbean Cruise Lines**, www.rccl.com.Tel. 866/562-7625
- **Celebrity Cruise Lines**, www.celebritycruises.com.Tel. 800/647-2251

Entry Regulations
There are a few necessary items and documents that all visitors must have with them in order to be admitted to Bermuda. Upon arrival at the airport or cruise ship terminal, you must be able to present your return flight or cruise ticket, proof of accommodations for the entire length of your stay, sufficient funds to cover your expenses, and a valid passport. If you intend to stay for over 30 days, you must also register with the Bermudian immigration officials. All visitors will be required to fill out a Customs Traveller Declaration form upon arrival.

Customs Upon Entry
Visitors to Bermuda are permitted to bring with them (duty free)

for personal use items such as clothing, jewellery, cameras, film, books, video cameras, laptop computers, sporting equipment, etc. They may also bring up to 50 cigars, 200 cigarettes, 1 pound of unrolled tobacco, 1 quart of liquor, 1 quart of wine, and gifts of less than $30 in value. All plants, live seafood, and fresh fruits and vegetables may be confiscated. Bermudian immigration and customs officials are famously suspicious of even the most harmless tourists, so don't be surprised if they ask plenty of questions!

After arriving at the international airport you will have a few (sometimes long) lines to wait on before clearing customs and immigration. If you are arriving by cruise ship, the passenger terminals also have customs and immigration officials awaiting your arrival and departure from the ship on a daily basis. Please bring your cruise ship boarding pass and your passport with you.

From the Airport to your Hotel
There are no rental cars available anywhere in Bermuda!

Once you have departed the airport, you can either take a taxi from the taxi stands directly in front of the airport to your hotel, or meet up with your prearranged transfer provider. Since there is only one exit, you will have no difficulty in finding a taxi or anyone who has been sent to pick you up. Taxis in Bermuda are metered, and the drivers are extremely polite and honest.

For a less expensive alternative to taking taxis from the airport to your hotel, there are two airport transfer providers that charge a fraction of the taxi rate. Keep in mind that the ride may be far from direct, as they may have to stop off at several hotels before reaching your specific destination, but with fares from $8.50 to $20 per person depending on the distance, this could add up to huge sav-

Avg. Airport Taxi Fares

- Airport to the city of **Hamilton** - $45
- Airport to the city of **St. George** - $27.50
- Airport to the **South Shore hotels** - $55
- Airport to the village of **Somerset** - $67.50
- Airport to the **Royal Naval Dockyard** - $70

ings. These transfers must be booked prior to your arrival in Bermuda.:

- **Bee Line Transport,** 3 Cahow Way, St. George, Tel. 441/ 293-0303
- **Bermuda Host Inc,** Hamilton, Pembroke, Tel. 441/ 293-1334

GETTING AROUND BERMUDA

Since rental cars are not available anywhere on Bermuda, there are several alternative forms of transportation available for use during your vacation. Almost all of the sights and beaches that visitors may wish to access can be easily reached by a combination of buses and ferries. Another popular way of zipping around the islands is to rent a moped or scooter. For those of you who would like a bit of pleasant exercise, renting a normal 21-speed bicycle might be more desirable.

Although not particularly inexpensive, it is also possible to take taxis from place to place during the course of your vacation. The following section will offer all of the current information needed to arrange your transportation needs while in Bermuda.

By Bus
The government of Bermuda's **Public Transportation Board (PTB)** has created an excellent public transportation system with 11 separate bus routes that crisscross the entire country. More than half the visitors to Bermuda use the Public Transport system during their trip. The PTB uses a zone system to divide Bermuda into 14 separate transit zones, each roughly two miles in length, which are used to determine what fare will be applicable to specific bus rides. To travel from one part of Bermuda to another it may often be necessary to travel through a few or more zones per ride in each direction. Currently the cash price (in coins only!) for all bus rides within 3 zones is $3 per person, while any ride through four or more zones will cost $4.50 (coins only!) per person.

Bulk 15 ticket booklets for multiple rides within 3 zones are $20, while the 15 ticket booklets for use on rides of up to 14 zones cost $30 each. You can also purchase discounted tokens at most hotels and Hamilton's main bus depot which cost $2.50 for 3 zones, or $4 for 14 zones.

Note: bus drivers do not make change, so have exact payment ready in coins, tokens, or passes before boarding!

For an even better price break consider the purchase of an unlimited use 14 zone (or less) pass which costs $12 for 1 day, $20 for 2 days, $28 for 3 days, $45 for 7 days, $55 for 1 month, and $135 for 3 months (reduced prices for kids available upon request. The above mentioned tokens, booklets, and passes are also valid for use on Bermuda's ferry system, described below, and can be purchased at the **Central Bus Terminal** just off Church Street in downtown Hamilton, as well as at several other sights including most post offices, Visitor's Service Bureaus, and leading hotels.

All PTB buses can be easily identified by their wide blue and pink striped exteriors and route number signs. Bus stops are located on various points throughout each route, and are marked with a pink and blue striped pole, and often contain a stone block waiting shelter. When looking for a bus stop, make sure that you are on the side of the street which will lead the bus in the desired direction. If the top color of the bus stop indication pole is painted pink then the bus is heading in the direction of Hamilton; if the top color of the pole is blue then the bus is traveling away from Hamilton. As you board the bus, tell the driver your final desti-nation, pay the required fare, and ask the driver to notify you when the bus is about to get to your stop. If you already know what stop to get out on, push one of the well marked "STOP" buttons located between the windows on the inside of the bus and the driver will pullover at the next stop.

All of the PTB buses start or finish their routes at the Central Bus Terminal in the heart of Hamilton (just next to the city hall). In some cases it might be necessary to make a transfer at this station to complete your journey. If you have to transfer to another bus, when you first board the bus and announce your final destination, the driver will provide a free transfer pass valid only for the next possible connection.

Most public buses usually run from about 6am until either 6:40pm or in some cases until 11pm. Buses do not operate late at night, and have limited Sunday and holiday schedules. Pay close attention to the timetables or you may get stuck taking a rather expensive long haul taxi ride (I got hit with an unexpected $70 one way taxi fare from St. David's to Somerset because I was one minute late for the last bus).

Bus drivers are not permitted to allow passengers with luggage to board their buses, so don't even think about taking one from the airport! The best source for detailed bus timetables and route maps is the free PTB bus and ferry schedule/map, available at major bus terminals, the Visitors Service Bureau, or the front desk of most hotels. *Info*: www.gov.bm. Tel. 441/292-3851 on weekdays during normal business hours.

By Ferry

Nowadays, with the recent addition of high speed catamaran ferries to the long standing regular ferry fleet, marine transport via ferry is a wonderful alternative to getting around Bermuda by other means such as scooter, buses, and expensive taxi fares. The ferry service is run by **SeaExpress** and is owned and operated by the Bermuda government. .

There are four ferry routes, and newer high-speed ferries also operate on several of these routes. Bermuda's largest and most utilized ferry station, known as the Hamilton Passenger Ferry Terminal, is located on Hamilton's waterfront just steps away from the intersection of Front Street and Queen Street. Here you can buy tokens and passes (cash is no longer accepted so please buy your tokens prior to boarding!) and pick up schedules and information. *Info*: www.seaexpress.bm. Hotline: Tel. 441/295-4506. Main Hamilton terminal hours are 6:30am-8pm on weekdays, 7:30am-6pm on Saturday, and 8:30am-6pm on Sunday.

A 1-day unlimited use travel pass is valid on all Bermuda bus & ferry routes and costs $12, the 3-day pass costs $28, the 7-day pass costs $45, and a 1 month pass costs $55. Single trip prices are different for some routes, which travel to and from the locations that follow:

The Pink Route (the slowest short haul ferry route) travels between Hamilton, Lower Ferry, Hodson's Ferry, Salt Kettle, Darrel's Wharf, and Belmont Ferry. No bikes or scooters are allowed on this ferry route. Tokens cost $2.50 per adult, $2 for local students, and 15 ticket booklets cost $20 for adults, $7.50 for local students. Seniors as well as kids less than 5 years old and local senior citizens travel for free. All fares are quoted on a 1-way basis.

The Blue Route (a slow medium haul ferry route) travels between Hamilton, Somerset Bridge, Cavello Bay Wharf, Watford Bridge, Boaz Island, and the Royal Naval Dockyard. Bikes and scooters are allowed on this ferry route during off-peak hours for a $4 surcharge. Tokens cost $4 per adult, $2 for local students, and 15 ticket booklets cost $30 for adults, $7.50 for local students. Kids less than 5 years old and local senior citizens travel for free. All fares are quoted on a 1-way basis.

The Green Route (a faster medium haul ferry route) travels between Hamilton and Rockaway. Bikes and scooters are allowed on this ferry route during off-peak hours for a $4 surcharge. Tokens cost $4 per adult, $2 for local students, and 15 ticket booklets cost $30 for adults, $7.50 for local students. Kids less than 5 years old and local senior citizens travel for free. All fares are quoted on a 1-way basis.

The Orange Route (a fast longer haul ferry route) travels between Hamilton and St. George and also offers service to the Royal Naval Dockyard (during High Season only). Bikes and scooters are allowed on this ferry route (excluding St. George) during off-peak hours for a $4 surcharge. Tokens cost $4 per adult (add another $4 if traveling between Hamilton and St. George), $2 for local students (add another $2 if traveling between Hamilton to St. George), and 15 ticket booklets cost $30 for adults, $7.50 for local students. Kids less than 5 years old and local senior citizens travel for free. All fares are quoted one a 1 way basis.

By Taxi

Bermuda has a large supply of 600 or so independently owned taxis, the majority of which are part of radio dispatch systems. In the summer, it is never a long wait to find a vacant taxi before 7pm, or you can summon one by phone. During the low season, drivers will often take other jobs, leading to a shortage of available taxis during rush hours and inclement weather. Many, but not all, taxis now accept most major credit cards. To catch a cab, look for an empty taxi and simply flag it down. Taxi stands can also be found at various locations, including Front Street and Church Street in Hamilton, King's Square in St George and at the Royal Naval Dockyard. Additionally, many of the larger resorts & hotels have dedicated taxi stands.

The newly calibrated taxi meters start at $6.40 for the first mile traveled, and add an additional $2.50 for each extra mile. This rate only applies to one through four passengers occupying the same taxi between 6am and 12 midnight from Monday through Saturday. If there are more than four people in the same taxi, the rate increases by a surcharge of about 25%. For each piece of normal luggage there will also be a $1 surcharge added to the meter. If you enter a taxi on Sundays, holidays, or any night between the hours of 12:01am and 5:59am the rate is also surcharged by an additional 25% or so. Taxi tour rates are $40 per hour for up to four passengers, and $55 per hour from five to six passengers.

Be advised that trying to find a taxi to take you back to your hotel after the clubs on Front Street close down at 3am or so is, at times, just impossible.

To call a taxi for a pick-up, contact one of the following companies:
• **Bermuda Radio Taxis**, Tel. 441/295-4141, 24 hours a day

- **Bermuda Taxi Operators**, Tel. 441/292-4175, 8am- 11pm
- **Bermuda Taxi Services**, Tel. 441/295-8294, 8am-11pm
- **Sandys Taxis**, Tel. 441/234-2344, 8am-11pm
- **B.I.U. Co-op Taxis**, Tel. 441/292-4476, 7am-12:01am

If you intend to do a lot of running around it may be best to hire a taxi driver as a tour guide by the hour at a flat rate of $40 per hour for one through four passengers, or $55 per hour for five or six passengers. Since so many of Bermuda's taxis are converted air conditioned maxivans, usually six people can easily fit in comfort. This is a great way for you to find out about the islands and get to lesser known attractions that may fit your specific interests. Almost every full time taxi driver is licensed and qualified as a tour guide. A blue flag on the hood of a taxi indicates that the driver is a qualified tour guide.

Avg. 1-Way Taxi Fares

- Hamilton to **St. George** - $47.50
- Hamilton to **South Shore Beaches** - $30
- Hamilton to **Somerset** - $52.50
- Hamilton to **Royal Naval Dockyard** - $67.50
- Hamilton to **Int'l Airport** - $45

I can recommend the drivers below for half- and full-day sightseeing trips anywhere in Bermuda. Call at least a day or two in advance and they can arrange everything from intensive specialty tours to sightseeing trips or private airport transfers:

- **Lenny Holder**, Taxi Van # 1826, Tel. 441/505-1826
- **Vince Cam**, Taxi Van # 1142, Tel. 441/234-7346
- **Michael Levon**, Taxi Van # 1299, Tel. 441/234-7268
- **Dennis Hollis**, Taxi Van # 1340, Tel. 441/234-8062
- **Mike Robinson**, Taxi Van # 1542, Tel. 441/737-3793

Let them know what you need, or if there is a tour or an airport run needed, and they will usually be right on-time. After finding a driver that you really like, ask him for his direct cell phone number for future use.

By Bicycle

For those of you who wish to keep fit while touring this beautiful country, I suggest renting a sturdy bicycle for use during some of your stay. The typical price structure for a 21 speed mountain bike is around $30 for 1 day, $55 for 2 days, $75 for 3 days, and $10 for each additional day. Expect to also get hit with a non-refundable repair waiver of $5 and a refundable deposit of around $10. The best places to rent bicycles include:

* **Dowlings Cycles** in St. George, Tel. 441/297-1614
* **Smatts Cycle Livery** in Southampton, Tel. 441/295-1180
* **Eve's Cycle Livery** in Paget, Tel. 441/236-6247
* **Georgiana Cycles** in Somerset, Tel. 441/234-2404

Or you can contact your hotel's front desk. Make sure to wear your helmet!

By Moped & Scooter

Moped and scooter rental agencies are located in hotels and branch offices throughout most parishes in Bermuda. The most common of these are gasoline-powered mopeds tend to utilize a 50cc engine which gets about 52 miles/gallon. If transportation for only one person is needed, a 3-horsepower moped will certainly do the trick. The least expensive of these one passenger mopeds have kick start pedals, and no electric turn signals.

If there are two people that would like to ride together, or a single person wants double the power and comfort of a moped, the 2-passenger scooters are the way to go. They have better brakes, stronger headlights, locking helmet storage compartments, lots of foot room, and a rear mounted metal basket to hold towels and personal items. All of these mopeds and scooters come with a helmet that must be worn with its chin strap tightened.

Unless otherwise indicated, there is a Bermuda-wide 35 kilometer (22 mile) per hour speed limit, although no one seems to drive this slow. Some people will tend to pass on blind curves, and several people are injured in avoidable accidents each season. Many of these accidents occur because the driver either didn't keep on the left side the street, or was looking at the bikini-laden beaches instead of the road. Children under 16 are not permitted to drive.

An important issue that the moped or scooter must be locked, and the key and helmet must be secured. Although third party liability insurance is included in all rates, this does not usually cover you against the theft of either the vehicle or helmet(s).

After some 50 or so miles, you will need to fill up at one of the many gas stations. Expect to pay about $5 per gallon and use normal gasoline. The typical business hours for gas stations are from about 7am until 8pm daily, but some stations stay open until 11pm. Bermuda has **only one 24-hour gas station**: the **Esso station** on Bermudiana Road at the edge of the city of Hamilton.

For one-day rentals, expect prices in the $50 range for a single or standard scooter, and about $65 for a double or deluxe scooter. Weekly rentals will set you back over $210 for single scooters, and about $250 for deluxe scooters. **Mandatory repair waiver (insurance) is $25**. Most of the following companies can arrange to pick you up and almost any Bermuda location:

- **Wheels Cycles**, (various locations throughout Bermuda). Tel. 441/292-2245
- **Oleander Cycles**, (various locations throughout Bermuda). Tel. 441/236-5235
- **Eve Cycle Livery**, (Paget, St. George, Int'l Airport). Tel. 441/236-6247
- **Smatt's Cycles**, (Hamilton and Southampton). Tel. 441/295-1180

BASIC INFORMATION

Babysitting Services
Almost every hotel and inn offers some sort of babysitting and child care service. Some of the major resorts offer in-house full day programs, others call in outside expert babysitters and nannies. *Info*: www.daycarebermuda.com.

Banking & Currency

The **Bermudian dollar is exactly equivalent in value to the US dollar** and is divided by 100 cents. While you can interchangeably use either currency (both are legal tender here) in Bermuda, you will have difficulties converting Bermudian dollars back into US or Canadian dollars once you have returned home. You can usually request that all change from purchases be given to you in US dollars only, thus avoiding the reconverting problem back home.

I strongly suggest that you use **traveler's checks** for added peace of mind. Now that American Express has doubled its fee to at least 2%, you should ask your bank if they offer another major brand such as Visa, Thomas Cook, Bank of America, or Barclays (sometimes banks will even waive the fee on these). In any case, you may be told that photo ID is unnecessary to cash these at shops, restaurants, hotels, and banks, but don't count on it! Make sure you have at least one piece of **photo ID** with you whenever attempting to use this method of payment.

There are no surcharges imposed for cashing travelers checks at most banks. Try to avoid getting denominations over $50 to make your life easier. Be sure to keep your serial number sheet separated from the checks in a safe place, and keep the 24-hour emergency refund number handy in case of theft or loss.

Bermuda has several large full service banks including the **Bank of Bermuda**, **Bank of Butterfield**, and **Bermuda Commercial**

Bank. These banks offer several branch offices which are usually open from 9:30 am- 3pm from Monday to Thursday, and 9:30am-4:30pm on Fridays. These banks can exchange most international currencies for a small fee, provide money orders, arrange emergency wire transfers, and cash traveler's checks.

There are also a variety of 24-hour **ATM banking machines** linked with the Cirrus, Plus, and Visa international networks for withdrawals from connected accounts (if you remember your PIN number). You can also find a bank at the airport that can be accessed from 11am until 4pm on weekdays.

Credit cards are widely accepted in Bermuda and most major resorts, shops, restaurants, and even some taxis will gladly accept Visa, Mastercard, and in some cases American Express. If you desire to pay your bill at a restaurant by credit card, use cash for tips if you can so your waiter or waitress will definitely get it!

Bars & Nightlife
The minimum drinking age is 18 years old. If you look somewhat younger than this, expect to be asked for picture ID. While pubs and bars usually do not have a cover charge, expect to pay a cover charge of up to $15 per person at most dance clubs or on weekend nights at venues with live music or DJs. Most pubs and bars have licenses that forbid them to stay open after 1am. Most nightclubs have special permits to stay open until 3am.

A few private clubs and after hour clubs may be open until sunrise, but you may have to be a member or an invited guest to get in. See my *Nightlife & Entertainment* section in Chapter 8 for specific listings on Bermuda's best bars and pubs.

Business Hours
Although this is beginning to change for the better, currently most stores in cosmopolitan areas such as Hamilton and St. George are usually open from about 9am until 5:30pm from Mondays to Saturdays. In the high season some tourist shops may open to at least 7pm, and during Harbour Night festivals until 9pm. Many of the shops at the Clocktower Mall near the Royal Naval Dockyard in Sandys are also open on Sundays.

Consulates

If you have a major problem that may necessitate a call to your government's representative for Bermuda (lost passport, crime, immigration difficulty, or arrest) these are the best contact numbers:

- **US Consulate General and Canadian Consulate General.** Both are located at 16 Middle Road, Devonshire, Tel. 441/295-1342.

Electricity

Electric current in Bermuda is **the same as in North America**. All outlets have 2 prongs, carry 120 volt - 60 hertz power, and do not require adapters or converters for consumer products from North America. If you're arriving from Europe, converters will be needed.

Laundry & Dry Cleaning Services

While most hotels and resorts offer their own in-house laundry and dry cleaning, the prices are extremely high. Since some of these places can pick up and deliver, a better idea may be to call or visit one of the following laundromats and dry cleaners:

- **Devonshire Laundromat**, 17 Watlington Rd., Devonshire, Tel. 441/236-7117
- **Duds & Suds**, 63 Middle Rd., Southampton, Tel. 441/234-2824
- **Quality Dry Cleaners**, Reid Street, Hamilton, Tel. 441/292-8193
- **Paget Dry Cleaners**, Lover's Lane, Paget, Tel. 441/236-5142
- **Warwick Laundromat**, Middle Rd., Warwick, Tel. 441/238-9692
- **West End Laundry**, 57 Somerset Rd., Somerset, Tel. 441/234-3402

Libraries

The **Bermuda Public Library** has its main location in Hamilton. Their hours are from 9:30am until 6pm Monday through Friday, and 10am until 5pm on Saturdays. There are branch offices in both Somerset and St. George's, open from 10am until 5pm on Monday, Wednesday, and Saturday. Visitors may make special arrangements to take out books during their stay; call for details. *Info*: Tel. 441/295-2905. Queen Street, Hamilton.

Mail Service

Bermuda has an excellent postal service with reasonable rates and beautiful stamps. You will pay only 70 cents for a post card or letter under 10 grams to go first class (usually by airmail) to the US or Canada, and 85 cents to Europe. The many branch post offices are generally open from 8am until 5pm weekdays only, but the **General Post Office** on Queen St.

in the city of Hamilton is open from 8am until 12 noon on Saturdays. The friendly postal employees can also sell many nice collectable commemorative stamps. There are also several private parcel and express package and document services in Bermuda including:

- **DHL**, Church Street, Hamilton, Tel. 441/295-3300
- **Federal Express**, Church Street, Hamilton, Tel. 441/295-3854
- **UPS**, Par-la-Ville Road, Hamilton, Tel. 441/292-6760
- **IBC**, Church Street, Hamilton, Tel. 441/295-2467

Medical Care & Emergencies

When an emergency comes up, call the **King Edward VII Memorial Hospital**, 7 Point Finger Road in Paget, Tel. 441/236-2345. They are open 24 hours per day and can also advise you on how to get a referral for specialists and outside doctors. The **Government Health Clinic** on Victoria Street in the city of Hamilton, Tel. 441/236-0224 may also be of some assistance in less urgent medical and dental matters.

You may find that your North American insurance policy may not cover all related expenses here. Please check with your insurance carrier for details.

There are many pharmacies scattered throughout Bermuda. You might be not be able to refill most prescriptions written by non Bermudian doctors. Late night pharmacies include:

- **The Phoenix Center**, Reid Street, Hamilton, Tel. 441/295-3838. Open 8am until 6pm Monday through Saturday; 12 noon until 6:30pm on Sundays.
- **Peoples Pharmacy**, Victoria Street, Hamilton, Tel. 441/292-7527. Open 10am until 6pm Monday through Saturday; 10am until 6pm on Sundays.
- **Collector's Hill Apothecary**, Collector's Hill, Smiths, Tel. 441/236-8664. Open from 8am until 8pm Monday through Saturday; 2pm until 9pm on Sundays.

Bermuda has just one number to contact the fire department, police department, and ambulances. In case of emergency, call 911.

Movies
Bermuda has a few cinemas usually showing first or second run American and English movies twice a day for about $9.50 each, although matinees may cost less. Exact listings and show times appear in the daily newspapers. Theaters include:

- **Liberty Theatre**, 49 Union Street, Hamilton, Tel. 441/292-7296
- **Liberty Theatre**, 30 Queen Street, Hamilton, Tel. 441/292-2135
- **New Somers Playhouse**, 37 Wellington St., St. George, Tel. 441/297-2821
- **Neptune Cinema**, Royal Naval Dockyard, Sandy's, Tel. 441/234-2923

Newpapers
Locally produced newspapers include the *Royal Gazette* (published Monday through Friday), the *Mid Ocean News* (published on Friday), the *Bermuda Sun* (published Friday), and the *Bermuda Times* (published biweekly). These are all available at hundreds of stores throughout the nation.

For those of you who crave news from home, a selection of international newspapers are flown in daily including *The Wall Street Journal*, *The New York Times*, *The Boston Globe*, *USA Today*, *The London Times*, *The International Herald Tribune*, and an assortment of other well- known periodicals.

Photographic Services

Film, camera supplies, and developing are all fairly expensive in Bermuda. The best bets for cameras and film development are:

* **Bermuda Photocraftsmen**, Reid Street, Hamilton, Tel. 441/ 295-2698
* **Sprint Prints**, Middle Road, Southampton, Tel. 441/238-3267
* **True Color Minilab**, Duke of York Street, St. George, Tel. 441/ 297-8024
* **Jiffy 2 Hour Photo**, Burnaby Street, Hamilton, Tel. 441/295-4436

Physically-Challenged Services

Accessibility laws do not exist for hotels, restaurants, shops, and public buses in Bermuda. Although some of these businesses do try and design a few special entrances and accommodations for wheelchair-bound clients, it is not that common. My best suggestion is to first contact the **Bermuda Physically Handicapped Association**, Tel. 441/292-5025. They may be able to help by providing a specially designed bus, pointing you to hotels and restaurants that have special facilities, and advising you on current conditions.

There is also a special transportation service offered by **London Taxi**, Tel. 441/292-3691; they maintain a hydraulic lift shuttle.

Public Holidays

On these days, most public and private offices, as well as many stores and business, do not open. The exact dates of these holidays vary each year, and may be slightly altered to create a three-day weekend. Public holidays include New Years Day, Good Friday (varies), Bermuda Day (May 24), The Queens Birthday (varies), Emancipation Day (varies), Somer's Day (varies), Labour Day (varies), Remembrance Day (November 11), Christmas Day (December 25), Boxing Day (December 26).

Radio & Television

Besides receiving several radio and TV stations from the east coast of America, Bermuda has several of its own. These include ZBM at 1340 AM, ZFB at 1230 AM, ZBM at 89 FM, ZFB at 95 FM,

Channel 7 ZFB (ABC), and Channel 9 ZBM (CBS). Most resorts offer a full range of additional cable and satellite stations from around the globe.

Safety Issues
Just like anywhere else in the world, Bermuda is not immune to crime. Since visitors laden with cash and jewelery make the easiest targets, I strongly suggest taking some logical precautions. Try not to leave your valuables, passport, airplane ticket, or cash anywhere but in a mini-safe or safety deposit box. Lock your moped each time you leave it. Carry a money pouch instead of a wallet. Keep your windows and patio doors locked at all times, even when you are sleeping in your room. Bring traveler's checks instead of cash, and try not to walk around the back side of Hamilton late at night.

Service Charges
In the vast majority of cases, **a service charge of 10%** is added to your hotel bill. This charge is divided up by the hotel's employees and eventually gets to people like bellmen, chamber maids, and other staff. Please try to leave a bit more for those who have gone out of their way to assist you. Additional charges like the so-called energy surcharge or resort levy may also be imposed on hotel bills. **Restaurants will often impose a 17% service charge** at the bottom of your bill. This also gets divided between the staff, but if the service is excellent, you may wish to leave a bit more.

Smoking
Smoking in Bermuda is **not allowed indoors** by shops, restaurants, bars, and offices, but it is still possible to smoke anywhere outside and on most patios and terrace areas. Most restaurants and bars have dedicated outdoor smoking areas.

Americans tend to go cigar crazy here and purchase Cuban products for their consumption while in Bermuda. While these cigars are illegal to import back to the US. Cuban cigars range in price from about $9 to over $28 a piece, and can be found at **Habanos** (on Front Street in downtown Hamilton), as well as at many trendy restaurants, bars, and tobacconists.

Those looking for American and Canadian name-brand cigarettes will find them for between $7 and $8.75 per pack at almost any hotel, restaurant, bar, gas station, or grocery shop.

Taxes

About the only taxes in Bermuda relevant to your visit are the **7.25% government hotel occupancy tax**, which is usual added to your hotel bill when you checkout, and the **$35 per person Bermuda departure tax** which may or may not already be included in your airplane ticket. Cruise ship passengers should be notified by the cruise line they are traveling with in regard to any port charges that may apply.

Telephones & Cellphones

This is one area where Bermuda is more advanced than just about any other destination I have visited. There are payphones all over the islands, and they come in different types. The newer digital display phones allow you to call locally or internationally by dialing first and then depositing coins as requested by a voice prompt or LCD readout on the phone itself, before the phone will place your call.

Local Bermuda to Bermuda calls via payphone cost 50 cents for each call of a maximum of 1 hour. You can also use the Bermuda Telephone Company **cash cards** (available at their offices and Visitors Service Bureaus), and make operator assisted collect and credit card calls. To call North America you must first dial the country code (1), the area code and the number. If you require operator assis-  tance for a collect or credit card call you must dial the operator (0), then the country code (1), then the area code and number you wish to reach. International calls are

Useful Phone Numbers

- Local Operator, 0
- International Operator, 01
- USA Country Code, 1
- Canada Country Code, 1
- Directory Assistance, 411
- Emergencies, 911
- Hamilton Police Station, 295-0011
- St. George's Police Station, 297-1122
- Somerset Police Station, 234-1010
- Air Sea Rescue, 297-1010
- King Edward VII Hospital, 236-2345
- Bermuda Government, 292-5998
- What's On in Bermuda, 974
- Weather Forecast, 977
- Current Weather, 977-1
- Marine Forecast, 977-2
- Storm Warnings, 977-3
- Time and Temperature, 909
- ATT Calling Card Access Code, 800/872-2881
- MCI Calling Card Access Code, 800/623-0484

cheapest between 11pm and 7am on weeknights. If you need to get through to an 800 number not in service from Bermuda, you may dial 900 – instead of 800 – and pay the normal long distance international rates to reach that line.

As for calling anywhere from your hotel room: don't! The surcharges are steep, really beyond belief.

There are three companies offering GSM, TDMA, or CDMA **cellular service** in Bermuda. These companies have limited contracts that in theory will allow US and Canadian visitors to roam in Bermuda using their North American-purchased phones, for a very steep roaming fee and special additional charges. I suggest contacting your service provider back home at least a week in advance of your arrival in Bermuda to find out the rates and special access numbers.

I usually visit one of several retail cellphone shops in Hamilton and I buy a cheap $45 to $95 model and then have the shop sell me a $20 prepaid cellphone card on the day I arrive in Bermuda and use pre-paid cell phone cards while I am on-island. All you need is an ID such as a drivers licence or a passport and you will have a number assigned to you on the spot. The shops even program the phones for you while you wait at no additional charge. While the per minute charges are high (upwards of 35 cents per local incoming and outgoing minute during peak hours and 25 cents per minute off peak).

You can also buy a TDI long distance phone card to use your cellphone to call outside Bermuda, and cards with additional minutes of prepaid local cellphone usage time can be purchased at many gas stations, pharmacies and grocery stores around Bermuda. You have no roaming fees to worry about. For local purchase, rental, and roaming details you can contact one of the companies below. Of the companies listed here, Cellular One has the best customer service and shop locations in Hamilton.

- **Cellular One**, Tel. 441/700-7600
- **BTC Mobility**, Tel. 441/295-4810
- **Telecom Bermuda**, Tel. 441/ 293-0550

One way to get around the high cost of calling your home or office from Bermuda is to buy one of the **prepaid phone cards** available in shops throughout Bermuda. Offered by local Bermuda based companies such as **TDI**, **North Rock Communications**, **Logic Communications**, **Cable & Wireless**, and **TeleBermuda**, plastic multiple usage prepaid long-distance phone cards can be purchased in denominations from $5 to $50 and can be used at any telephone or payphone in Bermuda. A typical call from Bermuda to North America will cost around 45 cents to 85 cents per minute using these prepaid cards. Most of these cards have toll free 800 access numbers in Bermuda, so you usually do not need to pay the 50 cent local call fee when using payphones.

Prepaid calling cards can be bought at any newsstand, Post Office, gift shop, and from a variety of vending machines and communication company offices in Hamilton as well as around the island. While a bit difficult to use at first, you will soon get the hang of it, and save plenty of money avoiding the hotel long distance charges which can run as high as $5 per minute in some of the larger resorts.

Time
The clocks here are set at Greenwich Mean Time minus 4 hours. This makes Bermuda **one hour ahead of the Eastern time zone** in North America. Each year, Bermuda follows daylight savings time between April and October.

Tipping
This is a matter of personal opinion, but I will give you mine. Even if your hotel posts a 10% service charge, I would still give a $1 per bag tip to a porter or bellman, $1.50 per night tip for the chambermaid, and a $3 tip to the concierge each time he reserves a tee off time or restaurant reservation for you.

In the bars and clubs it is usual to leave a $1 tip per drink. At restaurants that do not impose service charges, leave about 15% of the total bill. If they do impose a service charge, and you are rather impressed with their service, leave another 5% to 10% tip. If a sommelier (wine steward) is at all helpful, give him 5% of the bottle's cost.

Taxi drivers should get about 10% on the metered rate, unless they are not nice. For those of you on cruise ships, check with the cruise director for suggestions on tipping your service staff.

Tourist Information
The following are the locations and contact numbers for the Visitors Service Bureaus throughout Bermuda. Their hours vary from season to season, but you can usually reach them from 9am until 4pm Monday through Saturday.

- **Visitor Service Bureau**, Front Street, Hamilton, Tel. 441/296-1480

- **Visitor Service Bureau**, Kings Square, St. George, Tel. 441/297-1642
- **Visitor Service Bureau**, Royal Naval Dockyard, Tel. 441/234-3824
- **Visitor Service Bureau**, Somerset Branch, Tel. 441/234-1388
- **Visitor Service Bureau**, Bermuda Airport, Tel. 441/293-0736
- **Bermuda Department of Tourism**, 43 Church Street, Tel. 441/292-0023

Weddings

Visitors who wish to get married here must contact your local office of the Bermuda Department of Tourism to obtain a Notice of Intended Marriage. This form must be completed and sent several weeks in advance to the **Registrar General of Bermuda**. Along with the paperwork, you must send a bank check for $150 to cover the cost of the registration, license, and printed notices that will appear in Bermudian newspapers. *Info*: Registrar General of Bermuda, Government Registration Building, 30 Parliament Street, Hamilton HM12, Tel. 441/297-7709.

Civil weddings can be performed at the Registry General's office for an additional $150, or at any number of churches, halls, and private estates. For more information about private functions, contact **The Wedding Salon**, 51 Reid Street, Hamilton, Tel. 441/292-5677 or **The Bridal Suite**, Southampton, Tel. 441/238-0818. And some hotels offer wedding plans, such as the **Fairmont Southampton Princess Hotel** (*photo at right*).

When to Visit

Bermuda has two different seasons, both enjoyable – High Season and Low Season. Both are described below. Bear in mind that some months, like April in particular, can be iffy!

The **high season is typically April through October**. It is the warmest, most expensive, and busiest time of year here. Although the summer is fantastic in Bermuda, it does have both its advantages and drawbacks. During the day you can usually be more than comfortable with Bermuda shorts, sun dresses, polos, T-shirts, and perhaps a light water-repellant jacket in the evenings. The beaches are full, the seawater is warm, everything is open, restaurants can have long lines, the bars and nightclubs are packed to capacity, and the hotels and inns charge their highest rates. Some other holiday time periods such as Christmas and Thanksgiving time may also be considered high season.

While July and August can become somewhat hot for many people, September and October can bring occasional tropical storms and the odd hurricane.

However, it can still be rainy and/or cool in April. Even though the high season traditionally begins in April, you have a better shot at great weather **after mid-May** (see chart below).

Average Weather Conditions

	High Air Temp.	Low Air Temp.	Rainfall
January	67.8 F/19.9 C	58.8 F/14.9 C	5.85"
February	67.4 F/19.7 C	58.0 F/14.4 C	5.50"
March	68.3 F/20.2 C	59.2 F/15.1 C	4.55"
April	69.8 F/21.0 C	60.2 F/15.6 C	3.82"
May	74.7 F/23.7 C	65.9 F/18.8 C	3.19"
June	79.2 F/26.2 C	71.6 F/22.2 C	5.15"
July	83.9 F/28.8 C	74.6 F/23.7 C	4.75"
August	85.0 F/29.5 C	75.8 F/24.3 C	5.12"
September	83.1 F/28.4 C	74.0 F/23.3 C	5.76"
October	79.2 F/26.2 C	70.8 F/21.6 C	5.91"
November	74.1 F/23.4 C	66.3 F/19.1 C	4.23"
December	70.1 F/21.1 C	61.5 F/16.4 C	4.98"

The **low season usually is thought of as November through March**. The temperature is a bit cooler, you won't have to wait on long lines for restaurants, and bargains can be found everywhere. This time of year you can look forward to spring-like weather during the days, and chilly but refreshing winds in the evenings. The beaches are empty, the sea is a bit too cold to swim in, most hotels charge a fraction of their full rates, almost 50 restaurants slash their prices for a special dine around program, and a few tourist related businesses (such as a couple of hotels, restaurants, and most of the sea going excursions) close down. Now you may find some days where shorts are enough, or other days when you should consider wearing long pants, warm socks, a comfortable long or short sleeve shirt, and have a medium- weight water-repellent jacket handy.

This is still the perfect time of year for golf, tennis, hiking, museum, culture, and nature enthusiasts. It can also be rather enjoyable for those visitors who don't mind leaving without guaranteed sunburn. There are also many special activities which are offered only during this time of year such as free guided tours, social events, and open houses to private estates and their formal gardens. This is my favorite time to visit Bermuda, and I have often been surprised at how warm the weather can actually be.

What to Pack
Besides the appropriate clothing, you should bring several items which you may normally take for granted. Almost anything you need can be purchased in Bermuda, but at a premium. Consider bringing along personal hygiene items, a sweater for winter nights, a rainproof umbrella and jacket, a few good books, comfortable walking shoes, sneakers, appropriate golf or tennis shoes, swimming suits, beach towels, suntan lotion, a normal or video camera and perhaps a disposable underwater camera.

You might also want to bring along an alarm clock, a travel iron, batteries, a walkman, plenty of film, sports equipment such as golf clubs and tennis balls and racquets, snorkelling gear, a copy of any necessary prescriptions, an extra pair of contact lenses or glasses, sunglasses with UV coating, a money pouch, a water-proof key necklace, travelers checks, your ATM bank card, cigarettes (if you smoke, they are $7.50 a pack here), and if you are staying in an apartment you should bring allowable packaged and sealed food supplies. Since the electric current is the same as in North America, adapters and converters will be unnecessary.

Travel Medical Insurance
Since the possibility of a medical problem or accident is always a factor of risk, you may wish to take out an insurance policy. The best types of travel insurance are in the "Primary Coverage" category. In an emergency, most of these policies will provide 24-hour toll free help desks, lists of approved local specialist doctors, airlifting you to a hospital with the proper facilities for your condition, and much more valuable assistance including refunds on additional expenses and unused hotel nights.

Trip Cancellation & Interruption Insurance
Many special policies also cover vacation refunds if a family member gets ill and you must cancel your trip, if the airline you were supposed to be flying on goes out of business, if you must depart early from your trip due to sickness or death in the family,

if the airline fails to deliver your baggage on time, if the cruise ship which you are on comes back too late for you to catch your flight home, if your luggage is stolen, if your stay is extended due to injury, etc. Not normally covered are airplane schedule changes, missed connections, and flight cancellations. Check with your travel agent, tour operator, or the insurance companies for further details. In North America, try:

- **Mutual of Omaha** (Tele-Trip), Tel. 800/228-9792
- **Travel Guard**, Tel. 715/345-0505
- **Voyageur Insurance**, Tel. 905/793-9666
- **Access America**, Tel. 800/284-8300

INDEX

PHOTO CREDITS

The following photos are from Bermuda Department of Tourism: front cover and pp. 1, 13, 16, 17, 38, 39, 42, 43, 46, 47, 70, 145, 160, 168, 169, 205.

The following photos are from wikimedia commons: p. 32: Kongsvoll; p. 86: SeanMD80; p. 90: Mfdii.

The following photos are from www.hartleybermuda.com: p. 57. *The following photos are from Ron Charles*: pp. 56, 92, 109, 117.

The following images are from flickr.com: p. 9: FlyNutAA; pp. 10, 26, 27, 44, 69: walknboston; p. 19: zhengxu; p. 20: slgckgc; p. 35: djonemore; pp. 36, 54, 159, 185: Andrew Currie; p. 41: bg5000; pp. 48, 50: Paul McClure; p. 53: DharaHolistics; p. 64, 65: woofiegrrl; p. 67: urbansurvivor; back cover and pp. 5, 73, 79, 150, 178: Multiple fragments of tissue; p. 77, 215 bottom: antoaneta; pp. 80, 82, 95, 164, 170: Berd Whitlock; pp. 87, 88: midnight_narcissus; p. 98: Michelle K. Roach; p. 144: pieterjanviaene; p. 153: sim871; pp. 8, 161: rowland rick; p. 162: Zepfanman.com; p. 166: FuriousGeorge1; p. 179: wahoowadad; p. 197: ten safe frogs; p. 198: Cesar Vargas; p. 215 top: Canon in 2D.

Note: the use of these photos does not represent an endorsement of this book or any services listed within by any of the photographers listed above.

Things Change!

Phone numbers, prices, addresses, quality of service – all change. If you come across any new information, let us know. No item is too small! Contact us at :

jopenroad@aol.com

or

www.openroadguides.com

TravelNotes

Open Road Publishing

Open Road has launched **a great new idea in travel guides** that we call our *Best Of* series: matching the time you *really* have for your vacation with the right amount of information you need for your perfect trip! No fluff, just the best things to do and see, the best places to stay and eat. Includes one-day, weekend, one-week and two-week trip ideas. Now what could be more perfect than that?

Best Of Guides

Open Road's Best of Arizona, $14.95
Open Road's Best of The Florida Keys, $14.95
Open Road's Best of Las Vegas, $14.95
Open Road's Best of New York City, $14.95
Open Road's Best of Southern California, $14.95
Open Road's Best of Northern California, $14.95
Open Road's Best of the Bahamas, $14.95
Open Road's Best of Bermuda, $14.95
Open Road's Best of Belize, $14.95
Open Road's Best of Costa Rica, $14.95
Open Road's Best of Honduras, $14.95
Open Road's Best of Panama, $14.95
Open Road's Best of Guatemala, $14.95
Open Road's Best of Ireland, $14.95
Open Road's Best of Italy, $16.95
Open Road's Best of Paris, $12.95
Open Road's Best of Provence &
    The French Riviera, $14.95
Open Road's Best of Spain, $14.95

Family Travel Guides

Open Road's Italy with Kids, $16.95
Open Road's Paris with Kids, $16.95
Open Road's Caribbean with Kids, $14.95
Open Road's London with Kids, $14.95
Open Road's New York City with Kids, $14.95
Open Road's Best National Parks With Kids, $14.95
Open Road's Washington, DC with Kids, $14.95
Open Road's Hawaii with Kids, $14.95

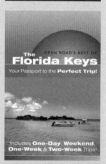

Order now at **www.openroadguides.com**